Knowledge Power

Success in the twenty-first century demands knowledge power – for individuals, organizations, cities, regions and countries. This book offers a map showing the structure of the knowledge space in a contemporary context. The routes beyond traditional disciplines are charted, in part based on the notions of superconcepts and superproblems. There are major implications for the development of education systems, particularly for universities but also for all employers as they seek to ensure that their organizations have the requisite knowledge to meet future challenges. In many instances, radical change is called for.

The traditional disciplines and their future development are reviewed and systems concepts are introduced to develop an interdisciplinary framework for the future. The nature of the knowledge core for different kinds of organization is outlined in the context of development strategies and management capabilities.

Superconcepts are introduced throughout and through these the reader is presented with a range of authors who, it is argued, provide the signposts for the way ahead.

Alan Wilson is currently Professor of Urban and Regional Systems in the Centre for Advanced Spatial Analysis at University College London and Chair of the Arts and Humanities Research Council. He was Vice-Chancellor of the University of Leeds from 1991–2004 and then Director-General for Higher Education at the (then) Department for Education and Skills. He is a Fellow of both the British Academy and the Royal Society, and was knighted for services to Higher Education in 2001.

D0322586

Knowledge Power

Interdisciplinary education for a complex world

Alan Wilson

Routledge
Taylor & Francis Group

LONDON AND NEW YORK

First published 2010
by Routledge
2 Park Square, Milton Park, Abingdon, Oxon, OX14 4RN

Simultaneously published in the USA and Canada
by Routledge
270 Madison Avenue, New York, NY 10016

Routledge is an imprint of the Taylor & Francis Group, an informa business

© 2010 Alan Wilson

Typeset in Galliard by Pindar NZ, Auckland, New Zealand
Printed and bound in Great Britain by TJ International Ltd,
Padstow, Cornwall

British Library Cataloguing in Publication Data
A catalogue record for this book is available from the British
Library

Library of Congress Cataloging-in-Publication Data
Wilson, A. G. (Alan Geoffrey), 1939-
Knowledge power : interdisciplinary education for a complex
world / Alan Wilson.
    p. cm.
  Includes bibliographical references.
  1. Education, Higher—Economic aspects. 2. Academic—industrial
collaboration. 3. Education and globalization. 4. Interdisciplinary
approach in education I. Title.
  LC65.W45 2010
  378.1'99—dc22   2009033336

ISBN10: 0-415-55310-5 (hbk)
ISBN10: 0-415-55311-3 (pbk)
ISBN10: 0-203-85803-4 (ebk)

ISBN13: 978-0-415-55310-0 (hbk)
ISBN13: 978-0-415-55311-7 (pbk)
ISBN13: 978-0-203-85803-5 (ebk)

Knowledge is power

Francis Bacon (1521–1626), *Religious Meditations*

Contents

Figures

Preface

This book stems from a belief that the structure of knowledge is changing more rapidly than is being taken into account in education and in a variety of organizations. As we all respond to experience, we build intellectual tool kits that we hope will enable us to be as effective as possible. The argument here reflects the building of my own tool kit over almost five decades as a researcher, academic, manager and consultant. There have been key authors in my life who have helped me to think things through and to build what I have hoped is a coherent framework for addressing a range of challenges. Intellectual tool kits are unique to each of us. The demonstration model offered here may provide a framework for others to extend their own kits.

In many ways, this book is about the fashionable concept of 'interdisciplinarity': why it is necessary to build knowledge power and what it means for traditional disciplines. It also gives me opportunity to reflect on the power of existing disciplines and whether this will slow down future development in universities in particular.

It is also about intellectual ambition, developing the capabilities – the knowledge power – for solving complex and seemingly intractable problems. For all the fruits of technology being available to us, there are enormous social, economic and political challenges to be faced. It is argued here that tools are available to meet a number of these – but they are not being used.

Over the last ten years or so I have lectured or given seminars on what I have seen to be the basis of knowledge power and superconcepts to a variety of audiences in the Universities of Leeds, Cambridge, Oxford and in my present 'home', University College London. I am grateful to those who have commented and asked challenging questions. This has all helped to shape the book. I am grateful to Joel Dearden for help with the figures and to Pion Ltd. for permission to adapt material from 'Science and the city', *Environment and Planning A*, December 2008, for use in section 4.7 of Chapter 4.

Alan Wilson
University College London
June 2009

Chapter 1

The knowledge challenge

All economies – both local and national – function in a highly competitive environment. The 2008–9 credit crunch has exposed the fragility of the global economy. Populations are socially polarized – intranationally and internationally. There are significant challenges for public service delivery: in health and education, from care provision for the elderly, to providing adequate housing and transport infrastructure. The planning system should sustain 'good' cities. There are challenges of developing and maintaining civilized cultural vitality. We have the knowledge to resolve many of these issues but do not use it. We can create the requisite knowledge. This is the knowledge challenge. It will be met in large part through education, research and lifelong learning. The need for a revolution in education is at the heart of our argument.

1.1 The knowledge economy

We live at the centre of a knowledge explosion. Technological advance, in particular, is extraordinary. And yet we live in societies of enormous contrasts of wealth and poverty, and in which the challenge of providing good, ubiquitous public services is a seemingly impossible task. In the private sector, major corporations collapse with apparently unerring regularity. Crime is a major issue; the media dumbs down. There is too much that is uncivilized in too much behaviour. So what has gone wrong? Why doesn't the growth of knowledge sustain progress? There are two kinds of question – broadly, social and economic. How can the knowledge explosion be harnessed to enhance the lives of individuals? How can we manage things better in organizations in both the public and private sectors of the economy? What does this mean for communities?

It is commonly argued that knowledge is now the key capital resource. Universities are seen as economic instruments. Companies appoint chief knowledge officers. Knowledge is also the key social resource: it empowers people in a knowledge-based economy; it is what underpins any kind of critical thinking. It is *civilizing*. In a phrase, what counts is *knowledge power*. To respond to the big issues, we have to begin by asking fundamental questions. What constitutes knowledge? And from this understanding, what constitutes knowledge power? We need to think radically and unconventionally – to reposition ourselves – to generate knowledge power for the contemporary age, for the economy, for communities and for ourselves as individuals.

It is well understood that as economies advance, they shift from being based on agriculture to manufacturing, and then to services. Knowledge economies are post-service economies. More workers are knowledge workers – information processors. Successful companies and public organizations – successful urban, regional or national economies even – are those that marshal knowledge most effectively. Anderssen has argued that successful societies can be characterized as c-societies that have three key capacities (or capabilities)[1]: cognitive, creative[2] and communications. The cognitive represents the store of knowledge; the creative, new knowledge; and communications capacity is important for high levels of connection and hence for sharing and gaining access to knowledge. The first two seem obvious conditions for success; the third somewhat less so. But communications capacity is fundamental for two reasons: because of the global economy of knowledge and because it provides a means of handling the knowledge explosion.

It is helpful at this early stage to anticipate a later discussion and introduce the notion of superconcepts – part of the knowledge power tool kit. These will be highlighted as they are introduced:

> SC 1. C-societies and organizations with the following capabilities:
>> SC 1a: cognitive
>> SC 1b: creative
>> SC 1c: communications

The contemporary knowledge economy is in many respects obviously global, though as Giddens[3] has argued that, almost paradoxically, localization often accompanies globalization. Interestingly, at least in modern times, there has always been a global economy *of* knowledge. Universities through their products – whether graduates or books – are key nodes in that economy. This notion must then be coupled with that of the knowledge *explosion*: in recent times the rate of growth of knowledge has accelerated sharply. The way to keep up, therefore, from the perspective of any one node, is to be well connected to others: communications capacity provides the access.

However, this is only part of the battle. Even if well connected, it is necessary to handle the large volume: to filter and to be able to navigate. This is precisely what is difficult in the use of 'internet knowledge'. Search engines need to be intelligent, and they are not. And, as we will argue, deeper knowledge is rooted in concepts rather than 'facts'. We need, therefore, to understand the key elements of knowledge power. We need knowledge power to move beyond the 'facts' – data and information – and indeed, beyond the rigidities of conventional disciplines. We need to understand where knowledge derives from. We need continually to enhance what we have. The second step, therefore, in coping with the knowledge explosion is to generate an understanding of the structure of knowledge at a higher level.

There are huge challenges here. But also tremendous excitement. It is not only the volume of knowledge that is expanding, but there are also sea-changes[4] in the kinds of knowledge available to us. We need to understand the richness of what is now potentially available. We are offered glimpses of the depths of knowledge about our world through all the core disciplines of science – arts and humanities expand and the cultural industries are a growing part of the economy. There are major challenges in virtually all public services. Through knowledge power, these can be met. Individual lives can be enriched, economies can succeed in new ways and services can be transformed. A Utopian vision, but worth the battle!

Meeting the knowledge challenge will demand a revolution in the education system – not just the formal system at all levels, but also a commitment to continuing education and lifelong learning.

1.2 Definitions of knowledge

Our approach will be pragmatic rather than, in a formal sense, philosophical. The first thing to recognize, as we trailed earlier, is that knowledge not simply about 'facts'[5]; it is about *concepts as the elements of understanding*.[6] These elements will be combined into *theories* about aspects of the world. In many instances, it will then be possible formally to represent theories as *models* that constitute operational representations of our understanding. These elements combine to produce intelligence, capabilities and critical thinking.[7] They allow us to be ambitious in our thinking, to cope with the 'difficult'. They enable us to think things through. (It is all too easy to think of examples where consequences of actions and plans have not been thought through.) Bransford and Brown in *How People Learn*[8] usefully summarize this from an educationalist's perspective:

> Learning with understanding requires a deep foundation of factual information and knowledge organised in a schema or conceptual framework.

We need to recognize at the outset, of course, that there are different kinds of knowledge, in particular, the theoretical and the practical.[9] Knowledge can be seen as, conventionally, partitioned into disciplines (though these are, as we will see later, social coalitions to an extent) and in combinations of disciplines – thus constituting what is commonly called interdisciplinarity.[10] So a key part of the argument will be to chart out the map of knowledge and its principal conventional partitions that have evolved, in many cases, over centuries. This provides a platform for an exploration of interdisciplinary knowledge power. This analysis will contribute to the necessary *breadth* of understanding; it will provide signposts when we need to search. It can be the basis of a radical programme of development.

1.3 Knowledge power

Knowledge power derives from concepts, theories and models that provide the basis of understanding and enable us to handle *difficulty* and *complexity*. Intuitively, this suggests that we need both *breadth and depth* – what Isaiah Berlin called the *hedgehog and the fox*.[11] We need the breadth to be able to recognize the kind of problem we have and to be able to select the appropriate elements from our conceptual tool kit. We need the depth to be able to confront real difficulty. We need to handle the knowledge explosion. Does this make the task impossible? Is the tool kit too big to carry? Even in a single discipline, there is a lot to master. But we can search for the higher level. We will argue that there are *superconcepts* that cross disciplines and which contribute both to our depth of understanding and help us to navigate the breadth. Also, that there are *superproblems* – generic problems – which are not being tackled because the intellectual equipment we have is inadequate.

Building the idea of knowledge power poses questions about the *value* of different kinds of knowledge: how to make judgements about *interest* and *importance*. The judgements about interest are inevitably subjective; those about importance, perhaps less so. We can, for instance, relate importance to the economy, an organization, an individual or to employment. A critical question is: who needs to know what? Part of the breadth argument is that *we all need to know something about everything*, so that we can, in principle, muster the requisite tools. And the depth argument implies that we should have the capability to tackle the most difficult problems: *we need to know everything about something!* There are serious implications for education at all levels here. As the argument proceeds, we illustrate by example. This leads us to some conclusions about directions of change[12] and so we will be concerned with priorities – academic, personal and corporate.[13]

1.4 An education revolution for the knowledge economy

Education conserves, creates and communicates knowledge – the 3 Cs again in another context. Success in the knowledge economy means success in education and the context generated by the knowledge explosion, and the contemporary economy demands a revolution. This is particularly true for higher education but there are implications for schools as well. Education has always been instrumental in two dimensions: for the economy, but also for liberal personal development, which is the basis of a civilized society. A valuable framework for beginning to articulate this revolution is provided by Cisco's 2008 White Paper,[14] which was rooted in the thinking of educationalists around the world. The focus of that paper is on schools, but its core argument can be applied to universities, and indeed more widely, and hence to the prospective drivers of the education revolution.

The authors of the paper use the language of IT to describe progression in education system development: think of the shift from Web 1.0 to 2.0 – from enhanced computing and communication to something fundamentally different – the basis of collaborative technologies, for example. The Cisco authors characterize *education 1.0* as pre-reform traditional education, usually centrally organized with a curriculum driven in a didactic way. *Education 2.0* is a reformed system, which emphasizes teacher quality, a new curriculum, school accountability and effective leadership – all of which should be learner focused. This means devolution of authority to schools within a system in which the outputs of the school are measured, providing the basis of accountability. Leadership – headships – and teacher quality are vital elements.[15] This can be characterized in a shorthand as R(T, C, A, L): reform (R) to deliver teacher quality (T), an effective curriculum (C), accountability (A) in a devolved system and delivered in part through good leadership (L) at both school and system (governance) levels.

However, the authors ask the question: what is, or what could be, *education 3.0*, the next phase? They add three areas for this development: twenty-first century skills (S), new web-supported pedagogy (P) and maximizing the contribution of technology (Tech). The whole package, therefore, can be coded as {R(T, C, A, L), S, P, Tech}.

SC 2. The Cisco template:
　　　　{Reform (Teacher quality, Curriculum, Accountability, Leadership), Skills, Pedagogy, Technology}

The basis of knowledge power lies in curriculum and skills (C, S), but the achievement of this relies on T, L, P and Tech – teachers and their leaders, pedagogy as representing the means of delivery, supported by technology. At first sight, this is very supply-side driven, but the aim is to construct the system in a student-centred way. Our challenge is to interpret this kind of framework not only for schools, but also for universities, employers and employees, and for people in relation to their individual development. And for universities – and indeed other twenty-first century organizations – this means knowledge creation – research as well as teaching.

Some of the elements of the Cisco template are so important in their own right that we identify them as superconcepts for future use:

SC 3. Accountability
SC 4. Curriculum
SC 5. Leadership
SC 6. Pedagogy
SC 7. Skills
SC 8. Technology

How can we articulate what is needed to bring about a sea change in education? The key has to be an understanding of the knowledge base of education – at all levels and embracing research as well as teaching. This means exploring and understanding what curricula and associated skills sets might look like. We have to find a way of handling the knowledge explosion, of recognizing the importance of moving beyond traditional disciplines for many purposes – that is, interdisciplinarity. We have to be able to handle complexity and difficulty and this means knowledge in depth; but the solution to some kinds of problems will need breadth as well as depth. All this has to be made relevant for organizations of all kinds, for communities and for individuals.

Inevitably, what is offered in this book is biased by my own background and knowledge.[16] However, the intention is to present it in such a way that there is a general structure that will help the reader to relate to and add to the ideas, and to develop further his or her own intellectual tool kit. Everyone has an intellectual tool kit, of course. Knowledge power is about the enhancement of that tool kit for maximum effect. It is something that is very personal. What we aim to offer here is the beginnings of a route map to aid this development.

The idea of 'knowledge power' begs the question of what constitutes knowledge. We begin our journey, therefore, in Chapter 2 with an examination in more depth of what constitutes knowledge – the knowledge 'space'. We begin with disciplines, first reviewing something of the history of the formation of disciplines, noting the extent to which they are social coalitions (or what Tony Becher calls *academic tribes*[17]). There is a dual purpose here. Knowing a little about all disciplines contributes to the breadth dimension. And we need to have some understanding of past and present as a basis for exploring the likely – and desirable – transformations in the future. A subsidiary aim is to offer a guide to a very diverse literature that informs this discussion – classical and contemporary, specialized and general. There is a need to draw a variety of ideas together into a framework, and for there to be appropriate signposts.

It is appropriate at this stage to articulate some basic definitions, to try to develop notions of disciplines that are as objective as possible. Then we can start to examine post-discipline forms of knowledge – interdisciplinarity – and to approach the idea of superconcepts by identifying ideas that are applicable across disciplines. This begins to provide the basis for what can be called *conceptual capability*[18] as the source of thinking power. We will explore concepts as they are used in different disciplines: when they are the same; when different. We need to understand the basis of transferability of concepts between disciplines. This can be a very productive exploration and the source of great intellectual excitement, but there are also dangers of misuse.

Conceptual capability will provide the source of creative power, of what has sometimes been called lateral thinking.[19] It will add power to research programmes; it will add degrees of inventiveness. By assembling broad *frameworks*, we can more effectively confront the knowledge explosion and avoid the dangers of compartmentalization.

There are big issues here. Can we identify a class of important problems that needs this kind of imagination? Are there such powerful generic concepts? We will argue that the concepts of *system* and *model* are examples. We will develop further the notions of superconcepts and superproblems. The argument needs to be illustrated by example and so, having developed the general idea of the knowledge space in Chapter 2, we sample it, with particular reference to superconcepts and superproblems, in Chapter 3. In Chapter 4 we look ahead and review disciplinary and interdisciplinary knowledge bases in terms of directions and priorities for future development.

In Chapter 5 we attempt a different kind of synthesis by asking the following question in broad terms: what do we need to know in different kinds of situations? What constitutes *requisite* knowledge? We can then use this analysis to explore the idea of knowledge power, first in organizations, second for communities and third for individuals. Universities are special organizations for the knowledge economy and so we devote a chapter to their role (Chapter 6). They are key knowledge nodes, concerned fundamentally with the conservation, communication and creation of knowledge. If there is to be a sea change in education, it will be rooted in universities. As we will see, they face a major challenge. We then investigate the structure of knowledge in different kinds of organizations – and the extent to which it is practical rather than theoretical; the extent to which these structures are sector dependent. We do this in Chapter 7. Chapter 8 summarizes what has to be done to bring about a sea change.

1.5 Summary: what is to be achieved?

There is a simple core to the argument, though unpicking it will be quite complicated at times! The core runs like this. Future development, both social and economic, depends on knowledge. The volume of knowledge is expanding dramatically – the knowledge explosion – and the nature of knowledge is changing so that it does not easily fit into the traditional packages. Understanding all this provides the basis for building knowledge power – for individuals, organizations and for communities. This implies the need for a reformed education system, offering both breadth and depth and with some repackaging. It involves developing the idea of requisite knowledge – what is needed in a particular situation at a particular time and how to acquire it – targeted knowledge power! This will provide the basis for solving our most difficult problems and rising to our most significant challenges. It provides the basis for building intellectual tool kits that are fit for purpose in a new era.

Chapter 2

The knowledge space

We can think of knowledge as constituting a richly filled multidimensional space. We explore the elements of this space and how to draw the boundaries that represent traditional disciplines. This provides the basis for articulating interdisciplinarity and its necessity in confronting contemporary problems.

2.1 Introduction

There are many possible approaches to building knowledge power. Knowledge can be thought of as a large set of elements in a multidimensional space. The dimensions of that space are the means of classifying the elements – and there is no unique way of doing this. However, we do need to understand this space, and so we begin by exploring the traditional dimensions of classification provided by existing disciplines. This will lead us to an exploration of interdisciplinarity and a problem focus. It will give us the basis for moving from a nineteenth-century framework (and some twentieth) and associated disciplines to something new for the new century. We begin, however, with an analysis of traditional academic disciplines and the relations between them. First, we explore the different *kinds* of disciplines: abstract and enabling (section 2.2); and those defined in relation to major systems (2.3). Then under the first of two headings concerned with *knowledge in practice*, we outline those relating to the professions (2.4); and others that can be seen as specialist and have emerged from interdisciplinary work (2.5). In section 2.6 we have the second *knowledge in practice* heading, that relates to skills that are generic across all structures. All of this provides a platform for the discussion of interdisciplinarity and superconcepts (2.7) and this in turn, as we begin to define the basic 'dimensions', allows us to complete the description of the knowledge 'space' (2.8). This, of course, is not static and the changing knowledge agenda is discussed in section 2.9.[1] Some next steps are outlined in section 2.10.

Our objectives in this chapter are threefold:

1 to lay the foundations of understanding of the knowledge space;
2 to give some indication of *what we ought to know* in broad terms – the beginnings of the 'breadth' part of the 'breadth and depth' argument;

3   to be on the lookout for what might be developed as superconcepts –
notwithstanding their disciplinary origins.

2.2 Abstract and enabling disciplines

2.2.1 Introduction

There are some fundamentals in our knowledge base that should be articulated
at the outset:

- philosophy
- mathematics
- computer science.

Philosophy is the discipline that clarifies what we are about: what is true and
how we show something to be true; how to represent this knowledge in language. Concepts can be complicated, and their meanings can change over time.
So underpinning philosophies need to be extended into the realms of semiotics.[2] Mathematics provides a key tool with which to facilitate the representation
of much understanding in depth. Most of science would not exist in its present
advanced form without these underpinnings. This raises difficult questions for a
book of this kind. It has been argued that every algebraic equation in a book loses,
say, 1000 possible readers. And so there are no equations in this text but we risk a
mathematical appendix to give a flavour of what non-mathematicians are missing!
Computer science then has to be added to the mix. The power of computers has
enabled otherwise intractable problems to be solved but has also facilitated wider
access to understanding through, for example, the power of visualization.

2.2.2 Philosophy

Philosophy has a pervasive but usually implicit influence on the way we think and
the way we approach what constitutes knowledge.[3] This is territory that illustrates
the breadth and depth argument very well. We all need to know enough about
philosophy to have formulated our own intellectual underpinnings. There are
many, often competing sets of ideas, which could be pursued professionally and
in more depth. What is offered here are some ideas that might stimulate.

We begin by exploring types of knowledge, first through the ideas of the
German philosopher, Jurgen Habermas, which provide a framework.[4] He writes of
three kinds of knowledge: technical (concerned with work, the empirical and analytical sciences); practical (social interaction, intersubjective communication); and
emancipatory (ideology, power). A constant underlying question, where we need
the help of philosophy, is: what is true? Habermas has a surprising but illuminating
answer: *that truth is derived by consensus*. A little thought shows its plausibility.
That is how science works, for example. We know what is 'true' in physics because

we (or at least physicists) can agree about it; it is tested in an open society, and universities play a key role in this process. It is perhaps more interesting to look at areas of knowledge where we cannot typically agree: the arts, the social sciences, politics. Here we are involved in critical explorations. The consensus theory, then, is rooted in the idea of *communicative understanding* or what Habermas sometimes calls *intersubjective communication*. This 'consensus theory' is a key concept: it teaches us what is potentially controversial and what is not. This is a major aid to clarity of thinking and so we give it superconcept status.

SC 9. The consensus theory of truth

Perhaps it is this kind of understanding of the nature of truth – and that in many areas we will have to argue things out – that provides the basis of *tolerance* as a key value in universities. And in this respect, they can be models for the rest of society. This connects to the 'thinking things through' argument, which perhaps then also means 'arguing things through in a spirit of tolerance'. Note that in this context, tolerance is not simply about letting people do what they want, it is about critical and constructive social engagement.

These ideas were summarized by Habermas (as quoted by Bernstein[5]) as follows:

> The systematic sciences of social action, that is economics, sociology and political science, have the goal, as do the empirical-analytic sciences, of producing nomological knowledge. A critical social science, however, will not remain satisfied with this. It is concerned with going beyond this goal to determine when theoretical statements grasp invariant regularities of social action as such and when they express ideologically frozen relations of dependence that can in principle be transformed.

The Times Literary Supplement[6] in a review of Habermas's work asked whether he represented *realistic utopianism* or *utopian realism*! As we proceed, we open up more questions. Habermas's framework extends our earlier argument by suggesting that we need depth, breadth *and engagement*. This framework helps us to tackle the question: how are values determined?

In effect, he articulates the issue as the task of finding a set of common values. The values we might expect to find supporting higher education, for example, might include: understanding, mutual tolerance, democracy. In this last context, we have to worry about how to protect minorities; that is, how to deal with the problems of a selfish majority. This again raises questions about what is civilizing and civilized.

We can link Habermas's argument to Kant's categorical imperative: colloquially, 'do unto others as you would be done by'. More formally, everything you do should be justifiable as though it was a manifestation of a universal law. The *TLS* article[7] argues that Habermas has fallen back on Kant but has sought to make the imperative more active: the Kantian argument is argued to be based on *hypothetical* consent – presumably you think it through yourself and make a judgement. Habermas wanted this to be *actual* consent – through his emphasis on communication. Thus, in the Habermas model, values are determined through an evolutionary process of social interaction.

Values will, through the processes of communicative action, to an extent reflect society's values but can also have a major impact on them.[8] For higher education, this re-emphasizes the concept of engagement – presented earlier as 'communication' – as a key purpose. We have to recognize, then, that knowledge is *socially produced*. The Habermas argument is that we all have a *critical responsibility* to dig deep. We also have to recognize that the key value question associated with knowledge is: what is true?

So perhaps what is most important is the role of universities in these critical social processes – research, and teaching in an atmosphere of research, constant critical inquiry; not simply teaching from received texts; certainly being deeply suspicious of the idea of *facts*. It is this continuing critical assessment that gives universities such important broader roles in society – key nodes in networks of communicative action – and therefore key roles in the evolutionary processes through which values are determined.

2.2.3 Mathematics

The next step is to consider more fully two disciplines that are instrumental in many contemporary disciplines and so represent critical enabling 'technologies' – mathematics and computer science. (Here I include statistics and subjects such as operational research as subsidiary branches of mathematics.)

Mathematics underpins disciplines as diverse as physics and economics. In its own *pure* terms, it is abstract and represents our knowledge of relationships between abstractly defined entities. At this level, it will be understood by most people in terms of algebra or geometry – the former concerned with relations between variables (or 'unknowns'), the latter concerned with points, lines, curves and surfaces, and theorems that express the relationships between them. At deeper levels, these kinds of branches of mathematics are not as distinct as may appear at first sight. The most obvious elementary example is the algebraic representation of geometry as *coordinate* geometry.

In the context of this book, we are usually, but not quite always, more interested in *applied* mathematics. In this case, our concern is with the use of mathematical formalisms to *represent* theories of systems of interest in a variety of disciplines, not just, as traditionally, in physics. The tool kit of mathematics provides a major component of knowledge power. What is now happening is that more and more areas within disciplines once untouched by mathematics are being expanded – hitherto intractable problems are being solved. This in itself is the product of expanding mathematical power and of our ability to learn how to apply known concepts more innovatively. However, learning to do this is a non-trivial exercise – both because of the lack of appropriate mathematical skills and because it often needs an exercise in imagination to switch, for example, from one representation to another to bring new tools into play.[9]

We give an illustration of the power of algebraic description in Appendix 1. This demonstrates the economy by which very complex systems can be described. When these descriptions are further developed in particular contexts and used to represent theories, then the theorems and insights of pure mathematics can often be brought into play and we will see examples of this later.

Within mathematics, it is appropriate to include statistics as a discipline. However, the philosophical approaches are fundamentally different – essentially the deductive versus the inductive. When mathematics is used to represent a theory, the consequences of that theory are deduced from it and then tested against experiment – the so-called *hypothetico-deductive* method.[10] Statistics seeks to work the other way round – the *inductive* approach. The pure view is that knowledge is contained in the data and should be inferred from that data and this is what statistics does. It is then possible to infer theories or algebraic models. The problem is that very stringent criteria have to be satisfied to validate most statistical procedures and this is often very difficult to achieve. These approaches have sometimes divided disciplines into two. In economics, for example, there is a fairly sharp distinction between 'mathematical economics' and 'econometrics', with the two 'schools' not always actively engaged with each other. In practice, of course, the two approaches should not be seen as opposed – and this is a typical component of the 'knowledge power' argument: they are different elements of the tool kit, to be used as appropriate. Indeed, to take an obvious example, mathematical models have parameters that have to be estimated from data, and this is a statistical process. The understanding of the difference between the deductive (and then tested) approach and the inductive approach – and the corresponding difference between mathematics and statistics – is not well known and we give it superconcept status.

SC 10. The deductive/inductive, mathematics/statistics distinction

A particular branch of applied mathematics, noted earlier, is *operations research*. This came to prominence in the 1940s through formal approaches to optimizing logistics in the war. By the 1960s, it was a flourishing trade with a wide range of applications in its own journals and professional societies. In more recent times, it seems to have lost its label – though there is still an Operations Research profession within the British Civil Service. Its content is still there, however, within the broader context of applied mathematics. It includes such standard solutions to problems as finding the shortest route through a network[11] and the travelling salesman problem – finding the shortest route by which a salesman can visit each of a number of points. There are superconcepts lurking here and we develop these in Chapter 3. We should also add that perhaps most of these techniques have been absorbed into computer science as computer algorithms, and it is to this subject that we now turn.

2.2.4 Computer science

The second key enabling technology is computer science with an impact that is almost ubiquitous. Many of the applications are conceptually straightforward – many arise from computer visualization. In this sense, the computer and associated information systems represent a new medium, enormously extending the printed page. The information systems themselves are clever and powerful – generating interesting research problems of classification[12] and navigation. These systems have the potential to revolutionize many business processes – and indeed many such processes, airline booking systems for example, have already changed fundamentally. One manifestation in education – in its broadest sense – is the development of Wikipedia, which 'solves' the classification problem through extensive use of hyperlinks – which moves beyond the linearity of the text. More broadly, wikis provide the basis for collaboration through the internet – essentially an element of the basis of Web 2.0.[13]

SC 11. Beyond the linear – wikis and multidimensional classification

There is also an argument to be explored that the wiki concept – developed to facilitate collaboration – can become the basis of a new kind of educational resource.

However, in the interests of further developing knowledge power, we also need to recognize the next step in the argument: that computer science is enhancing the power of mathematics through simulation – using mathematical models – and this is generating another kind of revolution in many disciplines. Examples will be given later in the context of the disciplines in which they arise. We will also recognize that computer science has accelerated the development of a new kind of mathematics – the science of *algorithms* – the representation of mathematical processes on a computer.

As the adjective 'enabling' implies, if we are to build knowledge power, we need to draw on elements of these disciplines. There are no short cuts. We need to be reasonably competent philosophers, to be literate and to have some mathematical and computing skills!

2.3 The big systems

2.3.1 The core disciplines

It is convenient to begin with the idea of a 'system of interest' and to use this in defining disciplines from first principles. We can think of a system as a set of related elements, and some very obvious examples are physical, biological, environmental and economic and social systems. A little thought shows that our world can be articulated in terms of such (overlapping) systems. If physical objects are the primary focus in a well-defined system – say a gas in a container – then the system is in some sense purely physical and such systems constitute the subject matter of physics. If the elements are interacting and changing at a molecular level, then we have a chemical system and the subject matter of chemistry. If any of the elements are living – or are components of living systems – then we have a biological system. On a bigger scale, we would characterize a system of interacting climate, landscape and bioscape as an environmental system or ecosystem, though its physical elements would obey the laws of physics and chemistry and its living components the laws of biology. This is the sense in which systems 'overlap'. People and organizations interacting in a region, say, form an economic system. The common feature of interesting systems is that they are complex and, as we will see, in this sense, understudied. There is a tendency in academic research to simplify the focus as far as possible – particularly shifting to the most micro scale, the reductionist programme – and to neglect the different kinds of complex phenomena that systems exhibit. Moving beyond reductionism is a key component of a radical programme of developing knowledge power and the development of 'complexity science' – to be discussed in detail in the next chapter – is a sign that this need has been recognized.

SC 12. Systems of interest

A distinguishing feature in the definition of systems, and hence disciplines, is *scale* – particularly in the definition of subdisciplines. There can be extremes, for example in physics, illustrated by elementary particle physics on the one hand and cosmology on the other.

SC 13. Scale

So with this kind of preliminary analysis in mind, we can formally sketch out what we would expect to find as the basic disciplines, based on likely systems of interest:

- physical systems
    - physics
        » quantum to cosmological (astronomy)
    - chemistry
        » physical
        » inorganic
        » organic/biological
- biological systems
    - molecular biology (biophysics, biochemistry)
    - genetics
    - cellular biology
    - organisms: botany and zoology
    - ecology

- microbiology, pharmacology, physiology, anatomy, etc.
- earth and environmental systems
  - geology
  - physical geography
  - ecology
- human/social/economic/geographical systems
  - psychology
- sociology and social policy
- demography
  - politics
  - economics
  - anthropology
  - human geography
- arts and humanities
  - languages, literature and cultures
  - linguistics
  - English, French, etc.
  - history
  - archaeology
  - theology and religious studies
  - art
  - music
  - drama.

Note that the biological area is particularly complicated because of the number of subdisciplines it can generate through the different approaches to elements and scale. In university terms, these are likely to have been established as separate disciplines – each with its own professional society[14] – than has been the case, for example, in physics. Botany and zoology, for example, would have been regarded as very different fields but they are now drawn together through the common foundation of molecular biology.

We proceed by illustrating some of the 'sciences of the big systems' in more detail, bearing in mind our objectives of laying foundations, giving an indication of what we ought to know on the 'breadth' dimension of our tool kit and beginning the search for superconcepts.

2.3.2 Physics and chemistry

Physics is an extraordinary subject. It underpins all of the physical sciences and, in a sense, much of the biological sciences. Its big and unsolved problems cover the widest possible range of scales – from the cosmos at the largest to the ultimate constituents of matter at the tiniest. In the middle scales, say the terrestrial, we perceive ourselves as governed by Newton's laws – the laws of so-called classical physics. Beyond the Earth, Einstein's theory of relativity comes into play. In the micro subatomic and subnuclear worlds, the laws of quantum mechanics dominate. It is worth exploring the subject matter in some detail, partly for the breadth agenda, and partly because it will illustrate in later arguments the way in which concepts used in one fundamental discipline can be used more widely.

All matter, whether in gas, liquid or solid state, is made of atoms. An atom is made up of even more elementary units: a nucleus, which in turn is surrounded by a number of electrons. The electrons are 'elementary' – fundamental – particles but the nucleus is made up of protons and neutrons. These in turn, again, are made up of quarks. Quarks are a relatively recent discovery and so the protons and neutrons, which are observable in a way that quarks are not, are also deemed 'elementary'.

There is a sequence of atoms defined by the number of protons in the nucleus, which have to be matched by the number of orbiting electrons. This sequence of elements, and its enumeration and account of the properties of the different elements, is the subject of chemistry. Atoms can combine to form molecules and so much matter is made up of such molecules – again the subject matter of chemistry. It is at the level of the atom that we get our first glimpse of the fundamental forces of nature. There are four: the strong forces that hold nuclei together, the electromagnetic force that connects electrons to the nucleus, the gravitational force, and the weak force. The gravitational force is much weaker than the strong and electromagnetic forces at the atomic level and we will hear more of it shortly. The weak force governs some behaviour within the nucleus, particularly in relation to radioactivity, and again, more of this later.

At this initial stage, it suffices as a starting point to think of matter as made up of atoms and molecules coupled with the notion that the atoms are made up of nuclei – of protons and neutrons – and orbiting electrons. It is the number of electrons in the outer orbit of atoms that determine their chemical properties. The strong forces hold the nuclei together, the electromagnetic forces govern the orbits of the electrons. It will be a feature of the developing conceptual base that each of these concepts will be elaborated – and will become more complex – as the exposition progresses.

Atoms and molecules are so small that they are directly unobservable. We are obviously more familiar with the entities of everyday life – gases, liquids and solids. The relationships between these entities are governed by the laws of Newtonian mechanics, of electricity and magnetism and thermodynamics.

We can observe the 'stars' and learn to distinguish the planets in our own solar system, and our own star, the sun. We learn something of our own place in the universe when we recognize that it is made up of billions of galaxies, each containing billions of stars. Astronomers put some sort of order into all this for us. In this chapter, we will be concerned with the rudiments of astrophysics: the universe through time, onwards from the big bang; the energy sources of individual stars; the mechanics of the solar systems as planets orbit the sun. These rudiments will embrace all scales, from the nature of nuclear energy to the scale of the universe itself.

The first step towards building theory in physics is to seek explanations of the motions of observable objects. This theory was assembled by Newton in the seventeenth century. Folklore has it that he observed an apple falling to the ground and realized that a force must be the cause of this – the pull of gravity. There were also some bigger problems to solve. There was much empirical data on the motion of planets in the solar system and it was understood that their orbits were elliptical, but there was no explanation for this. Newton's laws provided the basis. There are three laws of motion to which we must add Newton's law of gravity. The usual statements are:

1   an object will remain at rest or move at constant velocity unless a resultant force acts on it;
2   net force = mass x acceleration;
3   for every force acting on an object, the object will exert an equal and opposite force;
4   between two masses, there will be a gravitational attraction proportional to each mass and inversely proportional to the square of the distance between them.

We need to pick out the key elements of these formulations in order to work towards a more intuitive understanding. An object has *mass*, which we actually experience on Earth as *weight*. An object in motion has *speed*, such as 50km/hour, and when this is associated with a direction this becomes a *velocity*. The first law then defines the effect of a force, the first part of the definition of a force: it is something that changes the motion of an object. It makes the object accelerate. The second law is perhaps best looked at the other way round, as generating acceleration. The third law is more of a puzzle. The 'equal and opposite' argument is fine provided the object exerting the force back is fixed in some way. If it is not fixed, there is a net force and the second law takes over. It is straightforward to understand this intuitively if one thinks of pushing an object.

Forces are generated in all sorts of ways: human beings pushing; a piston being pushed by a controlled explosion in the cylinder of a petrol engine. The gravitational force, one of the four fundamental forces, is of a different nature: it is always there! The weight we feel in our bodies is the gravitational pull of Earth. Beyond a certain distance from Earth, the effect declines to a point where astronauts feel 'weightless'.

Once these core concepts and laws had been assembled, together with some mathematical apparatus – the differential calculus – it was possible for Newton to demonstrate that planets orbited the sun in ellipses – to offer an explanation for Tycho Brahe's data and Kepler's analysis of it. This illustrates another feature of much science: to proceed by approximation. Newton treated each known planet and the sun as a two-body system because the mass of the sun is so great that the gravitational pull between planets can be neglected. As it turns out, the three-body problem is almost impossible to handle analytically in applied mathematics and the utility of the approximation is paramount.

SC 14. Simplification – simplify the picture of the system of interest as much as possible to get to the essence of any 'law'

Fred Hoyle captured this idea very succinctly: 'It seems to be an over-riding feature of all physical laws that they become more elegant, simpler in a way, as we get to know them better, but that their consequences become more varied and complex.'[15] Much of the following discussion relies on the concept of *energy*. A simple starting point is to begin at the macroscale and to think of the two kinds of mechanical energy. If an object is in motion, then it has *kinetic energy*. If it is in a position where, if disturbed, it can accelerate under gravitational force, this is *potential energy*. An aeroplane in flight has both kinetic and potential energy. At the microscale, atoms, molecules and electrons can all vibrate – as well as, in the case of atoms or molecules in a gas, have a velocity – and hence have kinetic energy. All forms of radiation, including light waves, represent the transmission of energy.

Chemical change can release energy and this creates the possibility of storing *chemical energy*, as in batteries, which can then be converted into electrical energy. Perhaps even more important, energy changes associated with chemical change are fundamental to the workings of living systems. Some elements – enriched uranium and plutonium – can be changed to release *atomic energy*. And nuclei can be split to release *nuclear energy*. These last two cases arise from the convertability of matter and energy.

SC 15. Energy

We noted that the electrons were bound to the nucleus by electromagnetic forces. Each proton has one unit of positive electric charge and each electron, one unit of negative charge. There is an attractive force between the charges that mirrors gravity in its form. In the atomic case, we have unit charges of opposite sign that give a force of attraction. If the charges are of the same sign, the force is one of repulsion. We can then introduce a concept which is very important in physics – that of a *field* of force – in this case, an electric field.

SC 16. Field (of force)

The attraction between a proton and an electron can be considered to result from the interaction between two force fields. The notion of a field is probably more commonly understood intuitively in the case of magnetic fields. If iron filings are scattered around a magnet then they will arrange themselves along the lines of the field. And of course, Earth has a magnetic field and this is the basis for the workings of compasses. In this case, there are positive and negative *magnetic poles* with positive attraction between poles of opposite sign and vice versa. Magnetic forces can easily be experienced with common magnets from toy shops! One of the great achievements of Faraday initially, and then Clerk Maxwell, was to unify the theory of electricity and magnetism.

SC 17. Interaction

In terms of everyday life, we probably all have reasonable intuitive ideas of energy, work, heat, volume, pressure and temperature. It is much more difficult, but interesting and challenging, to make them precise in scientific terms and to continue to maintain our intuitive understanding. We begin by considering a gas – as a simpler entity than a liquid or a solid. Consider a gas in a cylinder with a moveable 'end' through which the volume can be adjusted. For simplicity, let us think of the gas as made up of atoms – elements – such as hydrogen, oxygen or nitrogen. We can translate our everyday intuition to this situation. We have already considered the *volume* – determined by the position of the head. If the container wall conducted *heat*, and the gas was warmer than its surroundings, then the container would feel warm, heat would flow from the vessel and we would have a sense of its *temperature*, from simply warm to very hot. Or conversely, if the gas was cold, then heat would be drawn in from the surrounding atmosphere, would be conducted through the container, and the gas would begin to warm up. The hotter the gas was, the more we would think of it as containing higher *energy*. If we had to manually secure the head of the cylinder to avoid it pressing outwards – that is, apply a physical force – then we would have a sense of the higher *pressure* of the gas; or again, vice versa. If we pressed inwards to reduce the volume, by applying a force, then we would be doing *work* on the system.

The theory of thermodynamics is rooted in four laws. The first is called the 'zeroth' law because it was added some decades after the first three were in common use. It essentially establishes the concept of *equilibrium* – more of which later. The third law is about the system of interest, the gas in our case, approaching a state of maximum order as the temperature approaches absolute zero. But we are running ahead of ourselves: what we need in the first instance are the first and second laws. We follow Longair, who formulates the first law as:

- energy is conserved if heat is taken into account

and, for the second law, he cites two equivalent formulations due to Clausius and Kelvin respectively:

- no process is possible whose sole result is the transfer of heat from a colder to a hotter body (Clausius);
- no process is possible whose sole result is the complete conversion of heat into work (Kelvin).

In accord with our intuition, the first law tells us that energy is conserved but that there can be heat loss. This is particularly important in another sense: it is our first example of a *conservation law*.

SC 18. Conservation laws

For the second law, Clausius most obviously accords with our intuition: that heat cannot flow from cold to hot bodies; while Kelvin tells us that when we construct machines to do work based on heat transfer, we cannot expect to achieve 100 per cent efficiency. Again, there will be heat loss.

The second law can also be stated rather enigmatically at this stage as:

- entropy always increases

but of course this begs the question of what *entropy* means. This will turn out to be very important in our later discussions and an excellent example of a superconcept:

SC 19. Entropy

We are now at the point at which we can begin to turn our intuitive understanding into something closer to a scientific understanding, still considering our simple system of interest – the gas in a cylinder. We can think of the atoms or molecules making up the gas as particles. The energy of the gas is the sum of the kinetic energy of these particles. The higher the energy, the greater is the pressure and indeed, the temperature. The pressure is represented by the energetic particles colliding with the cylinder wall.

We considered our cylinder to be one that conducted heat. To make our concepts more precise, let us now consider two cylinders whose outer walls cannot conduct heat, but are brought together and joined by a section that can be removed.

Assume that one is more 'energetic' than the other and has a higher temperature. When the cylinders are connected, heat is a transfer of energy from the hotter cylinder to the cooler one. This process will continue until a new equilibrium is achieved (which will involve a temperature between the two starting temperatures). So what is heat? The flow of heat comes about through the collisions between the particles of the gas: the higher energy ones will transfer some of their kinetic energy to lower energy ones on average. (Think of a snooker ball colliding with a second stationary ball: the second ball acquires kinetic energy from the collision.)

We can conclude this subsection by whetting appetites for a deeper explanation of some of the laws of thermodynamics. This level of explanation was achieved by Boltzmann in the late nineteenth century. The energy of the gas is the sum of the kinetic energies of the constituent particles. Thus if we knew the distribution of the energies of individual particles, we would know the energy of the gas. The absolute essence of Boltzmann's idea is this: suppose we count the number of ways the particles can be put into a set of energy levels – each of these a microstate – that is, a distribution, and we call this W. Then we look for the maximum of W, and the distribution of energies that produces this maximum is the most probable. In effect, Boltzmann recognized that it was impossible to model the very large number of particles in a typical gas by Newtonian methods

– recall that the three-body problem is analytically impossible! – and he very cleverly introduced the idea of statistical averaging by counting the number of microstates, W. Hence, this approach to thermodynamics is called *statistical mechanics*.[16]

SC 20. (Boltzmann) statistical averaging as a means of simplification

We have carried the discussion forward using a gas as an illustration. In fact, we know that there are three states of matter: gas, liquid and solid. Typically, the same substance can exist in each of the three states at different temperatures. A particularly striking and valuable example is water: we are all familiar with ice, water and steam – and with the temperatures at which transitions take place. Indeed *temperature scales* are defined in relation to the freezing point and the boiling point of water: 0°C and 100°C respectively. The different states are called *phases* and the transition from one to another is a *phase transition*. It will turn out that this is one of the most powerful concepts in modern science and has applications well beyond the realms of physics.

SC 21. Phase transitions – sudden changes in structure at critical points

At this point, we have to tackle a major shift in our picture of the microworld and revise our model of the atom. The concepts are difficult at first sight, but exciting. We do this in two stages: pre and post the theory of relativity.

It is interesting in thinking about contemporary debates on ensuring the utility of scientific research, which usually neglect the possibility of fundamental discoveries arising from applied research, that the notion of *quanta* arose after Max Planck had been asked to do some research to make light bulbs more efficient. He was studying electromagnetic radiation and discovered that the energies observed in their spectra were discrete rather than continuous. Waves of frequency ν emitted energy in quanta of hν, where h is Planck's constant.

Bohr had by now a model of the atom with orbiting electrons and he too was puzzled by observations of quanta of energy omitted from excited (i.e. energized) atoms. He developed Planck's ideas (which had already been further developed by Einstein) to argue that the orbiting electrons were in discrete orbits, each representing particular energy levels. Planck's constant again measured the jumps from one to another. So, if energy was added to an atom, one or more of its electrons would 'jump' to higher energy levels.

There were other surprises to come and eventually it was recognized (first by de Broglie) that particles like electrons had to be considered as being simultaneously a particle and a wave; and that further, electromagnetic radiation, such as light, also had to be recognized as exhibiting particle-like behaviour. The (massless) 'particles' associated with light waves are known as *photons*. Thus, we had the notion of *wave-particle duality*.

A corollary of the picture that was building up was encapsulated in Heisenberg's *uncertainty principle*: that it was impossible to measure simultaneously the position and velocity of a particle – with Planck's constant determining the strength of this.[17]

SC 22. The uncertainty principle

This, however, does not translate literally beyond microscale physics.

We now have to picture an orbiting electron as being in one of a number of discrete possible orbits, but also behaving like a wave as well as like a particle. This is probably why, in many textbooks, atoms are described as nuclei surrounded by *electron clouds*. It should be emphasized that this new picture is all about the microworld, very short distances, again determined by Planck's constant. The macroworld can still, at this moment, be thought of as described by Newtonian *classical mechanics*, in contrast to what has become known as *quantum mechanics*.

So far, we have three elementary particles: the proton and the neutron, different numbers of these making up the nucleus, and the electron. We have understood something of the nature of orbiting electrons and that, in general, the positive electric changes of the protons in the nucleus are balanced by the negative charges of an equivalent number of electrons, and that the electromagnetic forces keep the electrons in their orbits. We must now extend the picture, particularly in relation to the nucleus, to begin to understand the strong forces that hold the nucleus together and extend our list of elementary particles.

There was one dramatic breakthrough in the 1930s, which showed how the development of theory can launch ideas that demand new experiments to seek verification. In 1928, Paul Dirac developed equations to describe the motions of electrons but observed that there were solutions to these equations that represented an equivalent but positively charged particle, which was named the positron. The particle was discovered by Anderson in 1936. These, and earlier discoveries such as Rutherford's of the proton, and all the later ones, arose from the analysis of collisions between particles and the use of detectors to identify the products of those collisions. In the earliest days, the particle beams were from *radioactive elements* – of which more later – then from cosmic rays, and then, from the 1950s, from particle accelerators. By the 1960s, an abundance of new elementary particles were discovered and, through the 1970s, a new theory showed that some of these were made up of other components, notably quarks.

It is significant that this subsection offers so many superconcepts. As we will see, these ideas in physics will generalize within the field that is increasingly called complexity science.

2.3.3 Biology

As in physics, there are fundamentally different branches of biology defined by scale. At the upper end, there are the animals and plants that we experience in everyday life and indeed there are systems of interacting elements of these – ecosystems – the subject matter of ecology. At the microscale, we have molecular biology, which has been transformed since the discovery of the structure of DNA in the 1950s. At intermediate scales, we have cells first and then the organs (the most complex of which is the brain), which are the elements of working systems – the physiology.

The starting point of a simple overview can be taken as the cell. The simplest living entities are single cells – as in the case of amoeba. The most complex – human beings – have billions of cells. Humans grow from a two-cell beginning. Cells 'learn' how to subdivide and new cells learn how to locate themselves. This information is programmed into the DNA, which is copied into every cell of an organism. An account of this growth process is the subject matter of developmental biology, as yet imperfectly understood.

Once cells and organs can be thought of as 'grown' or 'assembled', it is possible to study the physiology of the whole system: how it 'works'. For the sake of illustration, we will focus on humans. In essence, cells and organs need energy to function and this energy is derived from the processing of nutrients. The nutrients are taken from the wider environment into the body. Much of physiology can be understood from these flows. Within the body, the flow of blood, pumped by that key organ, the heart, plays a crucial role. The 'control system' is, of course, very complicated. The DNA molecules act as templates for the production of proteins and enzymes, which carry 'information' around the entity. The brain runs a control system at different levels – from the autonomic, for breathing for example, through to our ability for thought-based actions. Stafford Beer characterized the human nervous system as the 'most sophisticated system ever to evolve in nature' and we will further develop his view of it in Chapter 3.

There are further complications. The body can take in not just nutrients, but bacteria and viruses that cause disease, and the body's immune system marshalls forces – antibodies – to fight these invaders. Understanding the physiology, what can go wrong and what can be done to correct it, provides the scientific basis of medicine.

What are candidates for superconcept status in the argument so far? Consider:

SC 23. DNA as information carrier and development controller
SC 24. Hierarchical systems

It is easy to see from this sketch how the kinds of subdisciplines listed earlier can be identified. Molecular biology is an obvious example: that is, biology at the smallest scale, and this has become a huge industry since the discovery of the structure of DNA; and, of course, it has huge application in medicine. Genetics can then be seen as a sub-subdiscipline within molecular biology and has a history rooted in the works of scientists such as Mendel, that precedes the microlevel understanding. This perhaps illustrates the persistence of socially determined coalitions! Microbiology is concerned at a slightly larger scale with bacteria and viruses – and hence with infectious disease. Pharmacology is about intervention into molecular biology with drugs. At the macroscale, we move beyond using humans as an example in our sketch to considering the vast variety of species in botany and zoology and then to the interaction of species represented in ecology. We explore these last two fields in turn – especially because they are sources of some of the most important superconcepts.

How do we explain the variety of species? Darwin answered this question more than 150 years ago with the publication of *The origin of species*. The origins of life remain obscure: chemical reactions in the 'primordial soup'? But Darwin showed how the present variety could *evolve* over millions of years on the basis of a simple principle: the survival of the fittest.

SC 25. Evolution
SC 26. Principles of evolution – e.g. the survival of the fittest

Species interact and the study of these interactions is the subject matter of ecology. Again, we find examples of simple 'laws' that have complex consequences. As we noted earlier, all living things need nutrients – food – to convert to energy to survive. There are two initial concepts in ecology that have wider applications:

SC 27. Trophic levels
SC 28. Food chains

'Levels' are about scale, and interactions being between nearby or within trophic levels; the idea of the food chain is a consequence of this. Lotka and Volterra – independently – in the 1930s identified, in mathematical models, two main mechanisms of interaction: prey–predator and competition for resources. We will see in Chapter 3 that these turn out to have wide ranging applications across disciplines.

SC 29. Prey–predator interactions
SC 30. Competition for resources

2.3.4 Earth and environment: the beginnings of interdisciplinarity

The first question for geology is another evolutionary one: how did Earth evolve? We are in the realms of 'geological time' – millions, indeed billions of years. In more recent times, the shapes of the present continents and seas needed to be understood and the breakthrough came with the discovery of plate tectonics. This is probably not a superconcept except insofar as it serves as a 'shifting plates' metaphor to signify major change. Geology is important not only in relation to understanding Earth's structure but also because it is the discipline that interacts with evolutionary biology through the fossil record.

For more modern times, geology transforms into that branch of physical geography known as geomorphology: how physical processes, such as erosion by water or glaciers, shape the contemporary landscape. This is important, for example, in the understanding of river networks and flooding.

The environmental sciences draw all the relevant disciplines together to seek a comprehensive understanding. In particular, it adds biology and ecology back to geomorphology – and indeed chemistry and physics. Chemistry, for example, is important in relation to studies of the atmosphere and both chemistry and physics in relation to climate change. Since much of the contemporary environment has been shaped by human action, not just in recent times but also over many centuries, human ecology becomes an important part of the analysis – and this also draws in disciplines as apparently disparate at first sight as history and the social sciences. What we see in a comprehensive study of the environment – a fundamental 'big system' – is that an interdisciplinary approach is needed and we develop this argument more fully in Chapter 3.

2.3.5 Social sciences

The social sciences are concerned with communities and societies on scales that range from the individual to the global. These can be defined in many different ways: by space – the residents of a city, for example; by nationality – including the global diaspora of a nation whose members have been heavily engaged in outmigration; by ethnic group; by wealth; by organization – the workers in an industry, for example; or combinations of all these. The relevant disciplines are richly diverse in their approaches and we briefly explore their various perspectives. There are also considerable – actual and potential – overlaps with the humanities, particularly history. It is obvious from the outset – though not put into practice – that an interdisciplinary approach is likely to be more fruitful.

If we focus first on the individual, the relevant disciplinary starting point is psychology. This covers an enormous range, from the study of the behaviour of rats in controlled environments through attempts to understand the individual human psyche to group behaviour – social psychology – the last probably having some relationship with anthropology. Some of its foundations are rooted in a traditional kind of science, usually based on experiments and statistics; some in neurophysiology and attempts to relate parts of the brain to, say, human emotion; some are more speculative and less easily subject to test in the way this is usually understood.

At the community or society level, counting people is a starting point – formally the discipline of demography. This involves studying patterns of birth, death and migration rates at various geographical scales. The theory is pretty well developed and there are typically rich sources of data from national censuses, which also facilitates historical demography.

The discipline that is pre-eminently concerned with the study of societies is sociology and this, from a definitional perspective, could absorb all of the social sciences. In practice, however, its purview is more limited. It has obvious concerns with social classification – as in the various definitions of social class, social structures, social movements and change. Its theories embrace ideologies and power relations; its subject matter ranges from forms of industrial organization to crime. Politics could be a subdiscipline of sociology, but typically functions alone as an academic discipline – as 'political science', for example. It is concerned with government in the broadest sense – describing and understanding political systems – but also with public policy (though many other disciplines are concerned with this as well).

Economics plays a very distinctive role in the social sciences. Its subject matter is more or less self-evident: the production of goods and services in different kinds of systems – e.g. through markets – and all the measuring and theory building that goes with that. Conventionally, it operates at two scales: the micro and the macro. Microeconomics is concerned with individual (economic) behaviour and with the theory of the firm. In the former case, it is usually to postulate a utility function and to assume 'rational' behaviour and that utility is maximized. In a market system, firms are assumed to maximize profits. In practice, these models are very difficult to articulate. However, we can offer as key concepts

SC 31. Utility function and profit maximization

so that we can explore wider uses of these.

At the macroscale, national or regional economies are described and measured. The invention of the input–output model by Leontief in the 1960s is particularly important here and this provides a concept that can be used widely:

SC 32. Input–output model

It has become increasingly recognized that the assumptions of rational utility-maximizing or profit-maximizing behaviour do not reflect reality and there are various new movements based, for example, on imperfect information at the microlevel through to evolutionary approaches at the macroscale.

Human geography focuses on spatial analysis at a variety of scales – from the local to the global. The activities of people and organizations are studied in relation to spatial structures. The classical theories embrace the different land uses: agriculture, resource extraction and industrial location, (residential) urban structures and systems of cities in a country or a region. The antecedents of good theory go back to the early nineteenth century. Von Thunen showed that crop types were distributed in circles around a town, with the highest value crops nearest to the centre. He inferred this pattern from a theory of 'rent' that still underpins much contemporary theory.

SC 33. Rent and land value

Weber analysed the location of a firm in relation to its inputs – labour and resources – and its market, locating the firm at the least (transport) cost point within a triangle. Burgess and Hoyt, and Harris and Ullman, in different ways, articulated the bases of urban structure. Systems of settlements were constructed in a hierarchy by Christaller with his central place theory, largely based on market areas. All these approaches each share one characteristic: the system of interest is hugely simplified to make the analysis feasible. In the first two cases, monocentric systems achieve this; in the second, non-overlapping market areas. In practice of course, market areas overlap and systems are multicentric. These restrictions can all be removed with contemporary theory.

In the 1960s, human geography advanced to the point where it could be seen to be a quantitative science – and indeed, economics became more seriously quantitative around the same time. This development has continued, but the subject has bifurcated. The dominant stream has become more sociological and cultural, originally on the basis of Marxist theory – though this has become less fashionable since the fall of the Berlin Wall.

It becomes clear very quickly that when a system of interest is defined in geography, say a city and its region, then potentially knowledge from all the social science disciplines and indeed, humanities subjects such as history and the sciences that make up the environmental field, should be brought to bear. This approach exposes the fragmentation of the social sciences in fundamental respects and supports the need for an interdisciplinary approach.

2.3.6 Humanities and the creative arts

It seems intuitively obvious that we should maintain an effective knowledge of human history and this remains a popular and important humanities discipline. Much history is within the paradigm of what might be called evidence-based knowledge and there is almost a cult of writing history based on original sources – or, more usually, the addition of new sources to old. The process is cumulative and of a different nature to advances in science.

SC 34. Evidence-based knowledge

It then seems as though the representation of past cultures in literature is at another extreme – presented as fiction – and this takes us into the realm of the creative arts. Some fiction, of course, is about imagined worlds that bear no obvious resemblance to the real one – though in most cases, a metaphorical one. But 'realistic' fiction can offer deep insights into the nature of the world we live in. The same argument can be put for the other creative arts – painting, sculpture, music, theatre, cinema.

This raises the question of the relationship of the humanities to the arts. History and related disciplines such as archaeology and anthropology stand alone. They are more like science in terms of the nature of their knowledge. The study of fiction, however, as in the discipline, say of English literature, can then be seen as 'professional reflection'.[18]

The study of languages falls within the humanities brief – first through specialist disciplines such as linguistics or philology, second through the variety of languages, which are then usually studied in universities along with the associated literature and cultures.

The humanities tell us about the important things in life and this knowledge underpins public policy. Martha Nussbaum, in a paper for the AAU Centennial meeting at the University of Chicago in 2000, said:

> One thing my development work has shown me is that public policy made without the influence of the humanities is likely to be cramped and crude. The cultivation of the imagination that comes with the study of literature, the cultivation of ethical sensibility that comes with the study of philosophy and religion – these are essential equipment for citizens and policymakers in a world increasingly united and driven by the profit motive.[19]

2.3.7 Towards interdisciplinarity

Even a cursory analysis from this brief review shows that the picture of knowledge presented by the core disciplines is a very fragmented one. Physics and chemistry are pretty well defined – as is biology in one sense, though in that case there are many extant subdisciplines. The more extreme cases in this respect, however, are represented by the social sciences and the arts and humanities. Jurgen Mittelstrass argued the case very eloquently in presenting a paper at an Academia Europaea meeting in 2005, when the potential position of the humanities in the European Research Council was being discussed:[20]

- There is an urgent need to raise the profile of the humanities.
- The humanities have a problem with their *visibility* both in the public sphere and in the academic system itself, and they also have an *organizational* problem when compared with other sections of the academic system.
- There is a strong *trend toward isolation*. The estrangement that emerged between the natural sciences, the humanities, and the social sciences in the course of the development of modern academia repeats itself on a smaller scale between the various disciplines in the humanities.
- There is also a trend to *intradisciplinary isolation*. Linguistics dissociates itself from philology, the empirical science of human development from education, literary theory from literary history. What had originally been a common language among disciplines is fading away. Suddenly Babylon is everywhere in the humanities.
- Individual disciplines in the humanities are increasingly plagued by *paradigm shifts* (not always sufficiently protected from fashionable trends) or (even more irritating) by *simultaneous paradigm shifts*. In history such paradigms are, for example, social research and narrativity or, in philosophy, hermeneutics and philosophy of science. Here, too, common conceptions are beginning to

disappear. Schools compete with each other over the monopoly of definitions in individual disciplines.

- With their unfortunate love of their idealistic origins (at least within the tradition of the *Geisteswissenschaften* in Germany) and with their unclear relationship to the natural and social sciences, the humanities are becoming increasingly *undefinable*.

- The humanities are to an increasing extent unable to cope with the fact that they not only *study* culture but are also *part of* culture. The historical dimensions are becoming too large. The result is a *loss of effectiveness*.

- *Quality assessment* in the humanities also becomes a difficult enterprise of course. Wherever no common disciplinary guidelines exist, there are also no common standards of assessment.

- My thoughts were not meant to plunge us into any discouragement. They should rather make it clear that it is not just a matter of holding the doors of a European Research Council wide open for the humanities, but that the humanities must also do their homework in order to be able to enter that door with their academic heads held high.

A systems view of the subject matter of the social sciences and the arts and humanities would lead to a very different and fruitful synthesis. For example, historians study the same subject matter as social scientists and the two methodologies could be effectively combined.

2.4 Knowledge in practice 1: disciplines defined by profession

2.4.1 Introduction

The next step in the argument is to recognize that the core knowledge in these basic disciplines underpins application in professional disciplines. We can proceed on the same basis and work towards a list. When the 'systems' disciplines are deployed practically, this is usually in combination with other skills and these combinations generate professional disciplines. If physical systems are combined into machines and devices through processes of design, this generates the various disciplines of engineering. When biological knowledge is applied to problems of health, we have a range of disciplines, from medicine through pharmaceuticals to public health. The skills involved in running organizations generate another cluster of disciplines under the headings of government and business – or strategy, leadership and management, overlapping concepts that are not always easy to pin down. And there are many disciplines associated with services for individuals. There is a particular set of skills associated with *planning* – and planning itself is an important generic concept that has applications in most fields. It can be argued that planning is made up of three distinct kinds of activity, and that these involve very different kinds of thinking: policy, design and analysis.[21]

SC 35. Policy, design and analysis: three ways of thinking

Policy is concerned with the articulation of objectives – what the planning process aims to achieve; design is invention – problem-solving; and analysis provides the underpinning knowledge core.

On the basis of this preliminary analysis, we can list some professional disciplines:

- engineering
  - civil
  - mechanical
  - electronic and electrical
  - chemical
  - mineral
  - mining
  - environmental
  - transport
  - energy
  - software
  - process
  - systems
- cities and regions
  - economic development
  - architecture
  - planning, transport
- health
  - medicine
  - nursing and other related professions
  - dentistry
  - veterinary
  - health services research
  - pharmaceuticals
- education
  - schools
  - universities and colleges
  - trainers
- management – government and business
  - public policy
  - accountancy
  - human resource management
  - economics
  - management consultancy
- social
  - law
  - education

- – health
- – social policy and administration; government
- – social work
- – criminal justice
- performing and creative arts
  - – design.

Articulating the list and thinking about each element will show the interdisciplinary nature of each field. This raises major issues of the depth that can be achieved in the teaching of professional disciplines. We will also see that skills are needed which in some ways go beyond those of the analytical disciplines. There is likely to be a shift to a problem-solving focus – diagnosis in medicine, architecture for a new purpose or building a machine deploying new technologies. These skills of invention and design complement analytical skills. They are not easy to teach, nor are they given high priority in academic circles.[22] We have listed management as a separate area, although the practice of each professional area – civil engineers within a construction company or health services within a hospital – each needs specialist management. An interesting and important question is then: do professionals acquire the necessary management skills within their area, or are there professional managers who can work within the territory of any profession? This question is made more complicated by the fact that many organizations need the talents of a number of professions to function.

2.4.2 Engineering

The Engineering Council lists 36 different engineering institutions on its website. This is an indication of the fragmentation of the area showing that this is not simply an issue for the social sciences and the humanities! In our own list above, we have listed four major players at the top of the list and then give an indication of other areas. Civil engineers need to know all about structures and ensuring that they are safe. This includes a knowledge of 'materials science'. Mechanical engineers build machines. Electrical engineers supply power, and electronic engineers, computers and control systems. Even this kind of very simple sketch shows how both specialist and integrated 'systems' knowledge will be required in most applications' areas. This offers challenges for engineering education in particular. Should the early (university) years involve a course in 'general engineering', with later specialization (which would be the 'medical' model)? Or should there be specialization from the beginning? How do engineers acquire the necessary science?

It is potentially fruitful to adopt a systems view – and indeed this is what many engineering companies, aircraft manufacturers for example, actually do. What is the 'system of interest' – an aircraft, a ship, a transport system …? And then, what is the set of engineering skills needed in relation to that system? The answer to that question is likely to define a new subdiscipline.

2.4.3 Cities and regions

Cities and regions are very obviously important systems of interest. A large proportion of the world's population live in urban regions and it is vital that we understand them, that they 'work' as well as possible and that there should be some form of effective planning to help achieve this objective. This importance is recognized by the fact that there is nearly always a form of local government within a system of national government; there are professions such as 'town planning'. The social sciences in principle provide much of the scientific underpinning – as the physical sciences do for engineering – though, as we will see, the connection is not as effective as it might be.

Figure 2.1 characterizes the main elements of a city or region as a system of interest.

This shows a city economy – defined in a broad sense – delivering products, services and jobs to a population, which, in turn, provides the labour forces, consumes products and uses services. Cities are not islands, of course, and any analysis has to incorporate in- and out-commuting and trade and migration. There is a rich set of interactions mediated by the transport and communications systems. The study of such systems is richly interdisciplinary and indeed, as noted in the next section, this in turn has produced some specialist disciplines or subdisciplines. This richness makes it very hard to provide an adequate professional focus. The mayor and local government, and the city chief executive, all have to have a broad grasp and understanding of issues and possible solutions and plans. They will be supported by specialist professionals: town planners, urban (development) economists and transport engineers, for example. They will also relate to the professional providers of services that are seen as essentially public services, such as health, education and police.

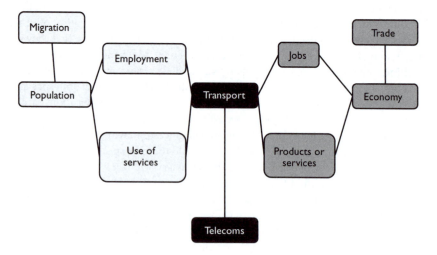

Figure 2.1 A city system.

2.4.4 Health

Health is a major industry staffed by a variety of professions such as medicine, dentistry, nursing, radiology and health service management. Most of these professions have to be underpinned by the associated core science and this is reflected, for example, in the length of education and training of medical doctors.

2.4.5 The social professions

There are major issues spanning through aspects of health care support care of the elderly through to prisons, probation and the criminal justice system under the banner of 'social work'. As with health, this is made up of a variety of professions.

2.4.6 Education

Education is another major industry, potentially spanning and contributing to all of us through a lifetime. We can distinguish – at various levels – schools, colleges and universities. The college and university schools of education have in turn to produce and sustain the teaching profession. They have to support, in the end, the kind of agenda advocated throughout this book.

2.4.7 Management: government and business

The third major professional industry is management in all its forms: government – local, regional, national, and international – and the wide range of businesses that make up the economy. From an education perspective, this has led to the mushrooming of business studies degrees.

2.4.8 Performing and creative arts

Actors, artists, dancers and musicians represent very different kinds of professions, each of which is supported by specialist degrees in universities – and often in specialist monotechnic institutions.

2.5 Specialist disciplines and the beginnings of interdisciplinarity

Specialist disciplines develop through combining elements of basic and professional systems to a particular focal point, a particular interest. Because of the combinatorial nature of the spectrum of possibilities, there are very many ways of doing this. Some particular examples are:[23]

- development studies
- European studies
- international studies
- food
- textiles
- colour
- transport
- communications.

These clearly involve combining elements of different basic disciplines, and it may be appropriate to characterize such approaches as multidisciplinary and to take this as the most elementary form of interdisciplinarity.[24] The first three of these are forms of area studies – defined by territory or focus. How does one know everything about an area, in terms of analysis and policy and planning? An undergraduate course can offer breadth but it would have to be very skilfully constructed in terms of later electives to offer depth. Someone could specialize in the economics of development but they would have to learn quite a lot of economics. The subject of food science defines itself. It is obviously demanding in terms of basic physics, chemistry, biochemistry and biology and relates to health, security and a host of other issues. Textiles is interesting in that it spans science and engineering through to business studies and fashion and design. Colour science demands a lot of chemistry and then knowledge of a very wide range of applications. Transport is a more well-established specialist discipline, usually located as a subdiscipline within an engineering faculty but also demanding knowledge of transport economics – and indeed development economics, city and regional planning and a chunk of other social sciences. Communications studies is analogous to transport, but is newer. It can embrace all the media on the one hand and the latest technology on the other.

There are some substantial questions in this territory: are we effective enough in delivering the interdisciplinary frameworks that are necessary? Can we find, for example, an interdisciplinary science course that embraces physics, chemistry and biology as a component of a number of these new specialisms?

Deeper forms of interdisciplinarity involve novel combinations of concepts, and it is this area that we explore in sections 2.7 onwards. First, we address the 'skills' issue.

2.6 Knowledge in practice 2: twenty-first century skills

It has always been recognized that there are skills that underpin all disciplines, indeed all knowledge: the ability to read and write effectively being obvious but important examples. In recent times, employers have called for 'communication' and 'team working' capabilities. There are now organizations that develop this kind of agenda for education purposes – a good example being the *Partnership for*

21st Century Skills based in Washington DC.[25] Their list includes:

- problem solving;
- decision making;
- creative and critical thinking;
- communication and collaboration;
- intellectual curiosity and the ability to find, select, structure and evaluate information.

They want learners who are motivated to be:

- independent self-starters who are responsible, persevering, self-regulating, reflective, self-evaluating and self-correcting.

This is a formidable list – the 'S' in the Cisco code. The development and nurturing of these skills complements the base of the knowledge challenge and is a key part of contemporary education development.

The linking of the skills and knowledge bases in education is itself a major issue. Most of the skills abilities in the partnership's list are ultimately dependent on depth of knowledge – what we will later call requisite knowledge. It can be argued, however, that the development of these skills, while initially motivated by employers, are complementary *and helpful* to academic development.

2.7 Interdisciplinarity and superconcepts

2.7.1 Interdisciplinarity

We have just seen some examples of interdisciplinarity that arise through the adoption of a *systems* focus – as in transport studies for example, which we saw involves mixtures of engineering (and hence mathematics, physics, etc.) and social sciences such as economics, geography and sociology. This type of interdisciplinarity may also be defined by big problems – superproblems – that demand a range of skills. Climate change is a current and topical example.

There is a second kind of interdisciplinarity that comes about through the *transferability of concepts*. Sometimes, as in the application of mathematics, this notion is second nature and is not typically thought of as interdisciplinary. This is why, in section 2.2 above, mathematics was characterized as one of the *enabling* disciplines. The notion of transferable concepts becomes more interesting when it is less obvious: when a concept that has been developed in one discipline can solve a problem in another (or an interdisciplinary problem). A key element of knowledge power is the ability to recognize this kind of possibility – in effect to recognize generic or superproblems – and to deploy the most powerful concepts that have been used, possibly in a particular discipline, to help in the solution of those problems.

This connects to the general issue in both research and learning raised in the previous chapter: breadth versus depth – the hedgehog and the fox. There are areas that fall between disciplines – or involve elements of many disciplines – which sometimes, as we saw in the previous section, grow into specialist disciplines. However, there is a *combinatorial problem* here: there are so many ways in which this could be done for systems of interest that this makes it impossible to define large numbers of sustainable specialist (sub)disciplines. *It is, therefore, one of the tasks of developing knowledge power to demonstrate how we can deal with this problem each time it arises – and this constitutes a strong statement about the nature of interdisciplinarity. Inevitably, problems in these areas are less well defined and the possibility of a tool kit of transferable concepts is the basis of a powerful idea.*

2.7.2 System and problem interdisciplinarity

An example of the first type of interdisciplinarity – the systems focus – encompasses much of industry through what has become a specialist academic discipline – business studies. Consider also fields like health studies (partly but imperfectly established as a discipline), pharmaceuticals or the cultural industries. Consider retail; business and management (involving elements of economics, geography, technology and engineering); aerospace and defence; automobiles; construction and building materials – all need systems approaches. Only one has become well represented as a specialist academic discipline: media studies. Or consider public policy: big systems such as cities[26], the environment and international development[27] demand interdisciplinary approaches. Most of the big strategic questions facing governments are of this type: education, health, crime, transport and so on. We will develop this agenda further in Chapter 4.

2.7.3 Conceptual interdisciplinarity

We can then move on to the second type of interdisciplinarity. From my own experience, an obvious example is the use of the concept of entropy – at the time I was first using it, almost wholly[28] associated with physics – to solve a problem in geography and transport studies: predicting person flows between origins and destinations. What ultimately emerged was that there is a generic class of problems solvable by these means that is still expanding rapidly.[29] While these approaches can be very fruitful and add to knowledge power, it is also possible to misapply concepts. Concepts like that of entropy, used to tackle a set of problems in a range of disciplines, can be thought of as 'above' – at a higher level than a single discipline – and hence 'supradisciplinary'. These are examples of superconcepts and we will expand on these ideas in Chapter 3.

2.8 Knowledge space

We can begin to collect together the ideas we have been exploring and elaborate the concept we introduced at the start of the chapter: 'knowledge space'. It is a multidimensional space with elements organized in some structures in that space. The most common of these structures are those represented by disciplines and combinations of disciplines – much of the latter formed out of practical experience. The initial and basic distinction is between abstract and enabling disciplines (section 2.2) and those, defined at a variety of scales, in relation to major systems (section 2.3). Knowledge can be combined into areas of professional practice and organized into associated disciplines (sections 2.4 and 2.6). Different combinations of ideas from disciplines generate interdisciplinary approaches and some of these form themselves as specialist disciplines (section 2.5). However, in section 2.7, we recognized that there is a combinatorial issue here: there are many more useful combinations than can be represented as specialist disciplines and this is the common basis of what is thought of as interdisciplinarity. But we went on to argue that there are superconcepts, which range across and above disciplines and add substantially to our knowledge power.

In summary, the power derives from concepts and theories from which we build capabilities – e.g. for handling difficulty and complexity. These include systems capabilities, problem-solving[30], issue-resolving capabilities, the analysis, design and policy capabilities discussed earlier.[31] All this relates to breadth and depth (again). Superconcepts in fact both broaden *and* deepen. We have to explore what this means, first through examples, and then through organizations.

We will also have to address questions of value. What is interesting – in terms of curiosity, difficulty, generating building blocks? What is important in terms of the *power* of a piece of research (both fundamental and applied) and the *range* of application (transferability)? We can try to distinguish between knowledge 'for its own sake' and generating productive capabilities. We need to chart out the big issues (fundamental, strategic, applied). We have to relate these ideas to those of creativity and rigour.[32]

It is an interesting challenge to try to be systematic about the structure of knowledge space, as Figure 2.2 illustrates.

This simple illustration cannot adequately represent the fact that this matrix is a huge though, to an extent, structured space. Our ongoing task throughout the book is to elaborate elements of this structure with two objectives: (a) to enhance our knowledge power in whatever circumstances any of us are called to apply it – and this has general implications for teaching and learning; and (b) to understand the dynamics – which has strong implications for research practice and policy. We briefly outline this second task in the rest of this chapter in preparation for a more detailed presentation in Chapters 3 and 4. Then we elaborate the structure of the knowledge space in Chapter 3, knowledge development in a variety of disciplines in Chapter 4 and in organizations in Chapter 5. We take on the

		Enabling disciplines		Concepts and theories	Superconcepts and theories
		Maths	Computer science		
System disciplines	Physics	*	*	Wave equation	Entropy
Specialist disciplines	Transport	*	*		*
Professional disciplines					
System interdisciplinary areas	Retail	*	*		*

Figure 2.2 Disciplines, concepts and theories.

challenge of devising action plans in a variety of particular kinds of organization in Chapters 6, 7 and 8.

2.9 The changing knowledge agenda

The structure of the knowledge space outlined in the previous section, of course, is not static. There will be some major shifts. It has been argued that we have reached, with say the human genome project, the end of science.[33] It is already implicit in the systems argument of this book that this is more like the (partial) end of reductionism.[34] This is a shift to a systems focus – and in particular to bigger systems at bigger scales. Some of the advances in knowledge power can come from reducing overriding compartmentalism. There are signs of such developments but the process is far from complete. We will be arguing, therefore, for more systematic thinking as the basis for major developments; for new links – for example, between biology and engineering and medicine in areas like tissue engineering. In particular, it will be important to focus on handling complex systems and in this context we will explore complexity science. Particularly significant in this context is the continued rise of mathematical modelling – deploying computer power and algorithmic thinking. This will not be an easy programme to implement, however, given the power of disciplines as social coalitions as recorded, for example, by Becher (1989)[35] and Bailey (1977).[36] We will have to explore the extent to which this can inhibit new thinking and our ability to respond to new challenges.

2.10 Next steps

We can now build on this preliminary analysis. In the next chapter, we begin to move seriously into interdisciplinarity and through the notions of systems and superconcepts. We begin to explore what might be emphasized in a twenty-first century curriculum. This is done on the basis of what we know now. In Chapter 4, we speculate on the future development of the knowledge base.

Chapter 3

Beyond disciplines

Systems and superconcepts

An important part of the tool kit in developing knowledge power, as we have seen from finding a way of defining disciplines, is the concept of a system. The next step in the argument is to explore the set of concepts that are applicable to many systems and in many disciplines – the superconcepts. This enables the development of knowledge power in a way that takes us productively beyond disciplines and will provide many of the enabling concepts for twenty-first century skills.

3.1 Introduction

It is already clear that the *system* concept is critical and generic – and can be adopted as one of the principal superconcepts.

SC 36. System

We have shown how the system idea can be used as the basis for a first-principles definition of disciplines and also how it will be a key to understanding the changing knowledge agenda – the shift from reductionism. Knowledge power depends on building the capability to understand *complex* systems. The systems approach forces us to be *interdisciplinary*. The system concept is an incredibly powerful one for enabling us to chart knowledge and understanding and to handle complexity. In this chapter, therefore, we focus in turn on systems and complexity (section 3.2) and on system models (section 3.3). Organizational models are particularly important and are treated in section 3.4. This is followed by sections on integration – relating complexity science to systems science (3.5), planning (3.6) and computers and algorithms – the underpinning technologies for system modelling (3.7). In conclusion, in section 3.8, we summarize through the concept of 'knowledge systems'.

This approach facilitates the development of the idea of superconcepts. The sections on complexity, models and algorithms each provide elements of a conceptual tool kit for systems analysis. The organizational models section is a special kind of look at generic structures of organizations as a preliminary for later discussions.

3.2 Systems and complexity

A 'system of interest' can be defined in the first instance by enumerating its elements – *entitation*.[1] The *location* of key elements is likely to be very important and it is the very essence of the systems approach to focus on relationships between elements – *interactions*. It is often important to count the different kinds of elements – a process of *accounting*.[2] It is also intuitively clear – and will become even clearer in the context of examples as the argument develops – that there is no unique way to *represent* systems. For example, we have already seen that we can use different scales in a hierarchy – most obviously, as we saw in physics, ranging from elementary particles to the cosmos. Representations are based on perceptions for specific purposes and there are nearly always alternative possible perspectives. It is important to choose what best fits a purpose: positioning a system in its environment, whether to be partial or comprehensive; scale; and, as we will see, in relation to concepts of fast and slow dynamics (structures, evolution and emergence).

The concepts of system representation, location, interaction, accounts, scales and hierarchy are all themselves superconcepts as will become fully clear as the argument proceeds. These are all listed here as important to this argument, but some have appeared earlier and so the previous number is given.

SC 37. System representation
SC 38. Location
SC 17. Interaction
SC 39. Accounts
SC 13. Scale
SC 24. Hierarchical systems

To fix ideas, consider cities and regions. We can identify all the elements of a city – a process we began in Chapter 2 with Figure 2.1, the entitation process – and represent it as a system at different scales – noting, for example, the population of a whole city; or subdividing into small census units. In the latter case, we can identify people by residential location or workplace location. The number travelling from one residential location to a workplace location is an *interaction*.[3] We can build population *accounts*.[4] If we enumerate the retail facilities in the city, we will find a *hierarchy*.[5]

One feature that makes systems interesting is their *complexity*.[6] Indeed, as we have already indicated, as we informally develop our ideas of what might constitute a twenty-first century curriculum, the idea of *complexity science* is an important one – and is already beginning to be in use in specialist centres in universities. Research councils now have explicit programmes in complexity science. We can easily have an intuitive idea of what constitutes complexity. A city is complex, but, as we will see later, through knowledge power properly applied we have more than the beginnings of understanding. The human brain is more complex and we are a long way from understanding its detailed functioning.

It is sometimes appropriate to complement our intuition by seeking measures of complexity. One important superconcept is that of entropy[7] (already introduced in Chapter 2 – and this can be used as a complexity measure). It was Ludwig Boltzmann in the late nineteenth century who formalized the use of the entropy concept in a particular way by relating it to the number of possible system states. A large number of possible states is a measure of complexity. The entropy is related to the logarithm of this number – which, in this instance, has the effect of turning very large numbers (of possible states) into a more manageable index. Again, this accords with our intuition about cities and the brain. We will see later that this can be related to the idea of information in a fundamental way. This was presented in the classical text by Shannon and Weaver[8] in communications theory, and, more generally, through Bayes' Theorem and Fisher information[9], both in statistics.

Another important idea can be connected to this measure of complexity: Ross Ashby's 'Law of Requisite Variety', which can be related directly to the idea of *control*.[10] 'Variety' in this context is given a technical meaning – which is actually the same as Boltzmann's: it is measured by the number of possible states of the system. This – and the associated law – are superconcepts par excellence with very wide application and which can be understood intuitively very easily. But Ashby's law is not well known! The basic idea is this: we often want to exercise a degree of control – the term is used technically – say, over systems through planning. A city with a local government that has planning controls – and perhaps a master plan – is an obvious example. Ashby's law then states that the controlling system – the planning system, in this instance – must have at least as much variety as the system it is trying to control in order to be effective. Once this is pointed out, it again accords with intuition. This is one reason why dictatorships usually fail. And also why they are repressive: the best chance of 'control' in this case is to simplify the system being controlled.

A valuable intuitive approach to complexity is provided by Weaver's classification of types of problem[11] – into those that are *simple*, of *disorganized complexity* or of *organized complexity*. Although originally formulated in terms of problems, the concepts can be directly applied to systems. Simple systems can be described by a small number of elements and relationships. We often still need the capability to deal with such systems – possibly even as components of more complex systems – Newton's laws, for example, in physics.[12] But what will turn out to be of particular importance for us is Weaver's distinction between disorganized and organized complexity. Complex systems have a large number of elements: in the case of disorganized systems, they interact weakly; in the case of organized systems, there are some strong interactions. The former can be tackled using Boltzmann-like entropy concepts; the latter takes us into more difficult territory that we pursue below in Chapter 4. We will give examples in the next subsection.

SC 40. Complexity
SC 41. Disorganized complexity
SC 42. Organized complexity

SC 19. Entropy
SC 43. Information
SC 44. Variety
SC 45. Requisite variety
SC 46. Control

It was in the 1950s when physics was undoubtedly the queen of the sciences, that Warren Weaver[13], with what turned out to be great prescience, identified his three types of problem in science – which we have just deployed to characterize systems as simple, those of disorganized complexity and those of organized complexity. He did this as science vice-president of the Rockefeller Foundation – seeking to provide an intellectual framework for ongoing funding policy. The analysis lead him to believe, rightly as it has turned out in many ways, that much of the future of fruitful investment in science lay with biology rather than physics. As he saw it, much of physics was concerned with simple or disorganized systems while biology was almost wholly about organized complex systems, which were much more challenging. However, we can illustrate his idea from physics.

As we have seen, a simple system is one that has few components, few degrees of freedom and can be characterized in terms of a few variables. It can typically be modelled algebraically through sets of equations that can be solved by conventional means. A complex system has many components and, typically, cannot be handled through conventional mathematics. However, the distinction between disorganized systems and organized ones turns out to be very important in this respect. As we have seen, a disorganized complex system has many elements, but they do not interact strongly with each other; in an organized system, there are strong interactions. He illustrated his ideas by a simple but effective metaphor. Consider a snooker table. If there are two balls on the table and one strikes the other, this is a simple system and the outcome of the collision can be modelled using Newtonian mechanics. If there are many balls on the table, the complexity defeats this mode of analysis (though the laws still apply). However, the balls are not strongly connected to each other. It is a system of disorganized complexity. Suppose now that many of the balls are connected by rubber bands. The set of interactions make this a system of organized complexity.

Weaver observed that, for the system of disorganized complexity, we have to ensure that we are asking the right question. Rather than seeking to model the behaviour – the paths in time – of each individual ball on the table, we might ask questions like: how often, on average does a ball strike a cushion? It turns out that this is a question that can be tackled – in fact, using the methods, mentioned in another context above, introduced by Boltzmann at the end of the nineteenth century for modelling the physics of gases. This field, as we noted earlier, became known as statistical mechanics. The atoms or molecules of a gas form a system of disorganized complexity – far too complicated to tackle by setting up Newtonian equations and attempting to solve them. But by using some new mathematics – of statistical averaging – the macroproperties of the gas can be calculated. Boltzmann, in effect, had introduced a superconcept that could be used beyond the confines of physics – though this breadth of use was not recognized for many decades. The key to the Boltzmann methodology can be seen as the maximization of entropy. It was only from the mid-1970s that the mathematics became available to help us handle organized complex systems – but more of this later.

3.3 System models

3.3.1 Introduction

When we have identified a system of interest, we usually want to represent our knowledge of it in some way. In many instances we can do this through the idea of a model as a formal representation of the system – and this becomes an important superconcept. It may be a qualitative verbal or diagrammatic description; a statistical or mathematical set of equations; a computer algorithm. Recall that there is no unique way of representing a system, and so there is no unique way of building a model. A good model has to represent our understanding of the system. It is a representation of our theory of the system. (Any theory would incorporate the known laws relating to the system.) If the model works, it will explain something about the system: how its structure has evolved; whether there is a steady state; more generally, the dynamics. In many ways, the concept of the model is more useful than that of a theory. It is the practical representation of a theory and this makes it clear the choice of representation of the theory should be explicit and should be thought about. We will find examples where there has been a historical reliance on a particular representation that is not necessarily the best for all purposes.

SC 47. (System) model
SC 48. Theory
SC 49. Understanding
SC 50. Explanation

The system model concept will dominate much of the future of science. It will revolutionize the approach to management and planning in relation to many complex problems. Consider the *simulator* argument. Aeroplanes, and the air space in which they fly, are complex systems. Pilots must navigate in such systems. They are trained on flight simulators and such a simulator is a system model. There are many other instances in which analogues of flight simulators would be valuable – but in most of these cases, there is no analogue of the flight simulator because there is no systems thinking. Examples will emerge as the argument proceeds – notably in the public sector.

SC 51. (Flight) simulators

3.3.2 Models in the core disciplines

Let us consider some examples. The most fundamental laws in science are the laws of physics. Critical elements of theory include Newtonian mechanics, quantum mechanics and the theory of relativity. Already, we can illustrate something about models and different representations that are appropriate for different purposes. For relatively simple systems at global macroscales, Newtonian mechanics is entirely appropriate. The mechanics and trajectories of space flight can be calculated on this basis, for example. Much of engineering involves models rooted in this way. However, at a microscale – the atomic or the nuclear – it is necessary to shift to quantum mechanics where the mathematics looks entirely different and represents concepts such as wave-particle duality and the uncertainty principle. The resulting model is of a different nature. At a cosmological scale, it is necessary to shift to the general theory of relativity, which is fundamentally different in another way. However, to complicate matters, there is an interaction between the scales: at the two extremes, the physics of matter in an individual star depends on the interactions of elementary particles and hence on quantum mechanics. There is an as yet unresolved theoretical challenge to develop a theory in physics – a model – that integrates quantum mechanics and the general theory of relativity.

The laws of chemistry are essentially built on the number of electrons in the outer orbits of atoms – more generally, on the interaction between electrons in molecular structures. In turn, the laws of biology at the microscale – in molecular biology – are built on those of physics and chemistry; at the macroscale – for plants or animals – there is system complexity of a different kind. Again, the two scales interact – for example, in the mechanisms of developmental biology and in the diagnosis and treatment of disease. As we have already seen there are some distinctive 'big system' problems associated with understanding the human brain. Biology has also been responsible, through Charles Darwin, for one of the most important superconcepts – that of evolution. This has an importance in virtually all disciplines and connects to the concept of *emergence,* which we discuss below. It is also interesting to note Deutsch's remark[14], in the context of knowledge power, that the evolution of knowledge 'resembles' biological evolution.

SC 25. Evolution

In the case of the social sciences, we should note at the outset that scale (cf. SC 6 above) also plays a critical role. The microscale is the single human being and the primary discipline at this scale, as we have seen in Chapter 2, is psychology. However, there is also the macroscale perspective through *social* psychology. Among all the sciences, its claim to objective knowledge has been the most contested, especially in areas such as psychotherapy.[15] Economics tends to divide into two scales – the micro and the macro. At the microlevel, the concern is with the individual or the organization, each typically assumed to have rational expectations so that laws can be formulated in such terms. At the macrolevel, the concern is with whole economies, most typically at the national level but sometimes at the urban or regional levels. There is an in-between level, which we might call the mesolevel, which is typically neglected. The models, representing the theories, at these different scales look very different. Sociology is less likely to be quantitative, but of all the social sciences, is connected to *structuralism*.[16] Human geography is distinguished by a concern with the spatial dimension of social and economic systems – and it is interesting that this is what distinguishes it, in the main, from economics or sociology.[17]

SC 52. Structuralism

The humanities are also concerned with both individuals – perhaps in the main – *and* societies. While literature is presented as fiction, it is clear that the novel, for example, is intended to represent a kind of understanding of the individuals represented and the societies of which they are a part; or to represent imagined possibilities. The creative arts are similarly connected to reality, but also, perhaps, to an imaginative representation of what could be in various circumstances.

The different disciplines, therefore, all have their models (and theories) – whether they are called models or not. It is from this disciplinary base that we can collect together the relevant knowledge represented in the laws that have been articulated. We will draw on these bodies of knowledge as appropriate to build interdisciplinary system models. The next step in the argument is to examine the generic nature of some of the models that have evolved.

3.3.3 Account-based models

A good general principle is to count system elements and to track these elements – through counts – over time. This is what accountants do with money for systems of interest to them – say, a company – and so such models are called account-based models. Some progress can then often be made by applying *conservation* principles: elements have to be somewhere, and accounted for, subject to processes such as birth, death and migration. These have obvious meanings in demography[18] and economics – in the latter case in the context of input–output models of economies at various scales – usually national[19], but also in the sciences like physics and chemistry where conservation laws play important roles. The appropriate superconcepts have each appeared earlier.

SC 39. Accounts
SC 18. Conservation laws

Much of the financial services industry depends on the work of actuaries whose 'theory' is rooted in demographic models. Equally, governments at all scales need to understand and to be able to forecast the (changing) demands for public services. In the case of economic development, a good understanding through input–output models would help to identify the importance of clusters and other such development triggers. At present, these techniques are scarcely used.

3.3.4 Optimization

Many models are expressed in terms of the maximization or minimization of something. Generically, and in a technical rather than a colloquial sense, both processes can be described as optimization. We described a number of examples in relation to operations research in Chapter 2. Sometimes, the structure of a system (or a problem) can be represented as *constraints* and then we can have *optimization subject to constraints*. The mathematics of these kinds of problems, as we saw earlier – and there are many types – have been well worked out since the 1940s[20], though some of the key elements go back in time to Lagrange. Many of the laws of physics are formulated in these terms. Microeconomics is founded on the notions of the firm maximizing profits and the consumer maximizing utility. The representation of constraints in these systems is often a key element in representing our knowledge of the system.

SC 53. Optimization
SC 54. Constraints, as representing system knowledge

As a simple example, consider the assignment of patients to hospitals. The constraints of the task would be represented by the numbers of patients to be treated by residential location and the treatment capacities of hospitals by location. The optimization problem would be to minimize total travel from the patients' perspectives. This can be solved as a mathematical programming problem. These concepts can be used in much socio-economic and geographic planning, for instance, in relation to transport and retail systems.

3.3.5 Combinatorics

Optimization problems often involve a procedure for identifying a 'solution' – perhaps an equilibrium solution – to a set of equations that represents the system or model. In physics, this may be the shape of a particular polymer molecule. In geography and marketing, it might be the identification of an optimal branch network for a retailer. It is possible to recognize intuitively – say, for this last example – that this is a combinatorial problem. Suppose the question is: how best to locate 20 stores in a network of 100 towns? There are $100!/80!20!$ ways of doing this – a very large number. This is a combinatorial problem. It is important to be able to recognize different types of such problems. In well-defined cases, the optimization procedure can identify a single best – optimum – solution. Even in those cases, it is important to know whether the optimum is much better than other 'nearby' solutions. If this turns out not to be the case, then we can begin to see possible real instances where the best can be the enemy of the good.

It is also now known that there are cases where even if there is known to be an optimum, there is no computing procedure that can find the solution in a reasonable time.[21] Deutsch (1997) might argue that this means no conventional computing procedure. In his work, he laid the foundations of quantum computing (which we return to in the next chapter). He envisages situations where there are 10^{500} possible 'states' to search – and to put this into context, it is estimated that there are 10^{80} atoms in the universe. But, he argues, quantum computing can handle this!

Even more interesting are cases where there is no unique solution – and this characterizes much of reality![22]

There may be laws to show that it may be possible to formulate a model; it may be possible to formulate an optimization problem, the outcome of which is an equilibrium. Think of the retail example again. It is possible to model the configuration of retail centres in a city – their locations and relative sizes.[23] However, it turns out that there is no unique solution. In many cases, there are many possible solutions. If the example is a real one, what actually determines the actual outcome? The answer is that there will be something that fixes the solution – perhaps a particular human act – by an entrepreneur or a planner. This links to what Arthur[24] has called *path dependent* development, which we will consider further under the heading of dynamics below. Thus, development problems in fields as diverse as biology and geography may be rooted in combinatorics.[25]

The optimization problems we have described are essentially search problems – that is, part of a wider class of problems. These occur in a variety of forms: the intelligent structuring and navigation of large databases; pattern recognition – the task of identifying a point pattern by matching it against one of a large set of known patterns, for example. This is closely related to the computer vision issue. Combinatorics is the science of these different kinds of 'large number' problems.[26,27] In a contemporary management context (management information systems), data mining also represents a kind of search.[28]

SC 55. Pattern recognition

This is a convenient point to re-emphasize the simple, but powerful, superconcept introduced earlier (SC 22) – that of *constraints*. If it is possible to specify constraints that must be satisfied by the variables which describe a system, then this reduces the size of the state space – the number of configurations the system can attain. This then reduces the scale of the combinatorial problem if the model is being constricted from an optimization process.[29]

SC 55. Combinatorics
SC 57. Multiple equilibria
SC 58. Path dependence

3.3.6 Models and the challenge of missing data

There is an important connection between data and models that can be picked up at this stage. If a model represents a good understanding and representation of some system of interest, then it can usually be calibrated in a particular case using, typically, a number of partial data sets related to the system. The model can then be used to 'predict', for the current time say, all the variables representing the system. In effect it has integrated the partial data sets – and indeed in many cases can estimate otherwise missing data. This ability to build more comprehensive data sets – better described as information or knowledge systems – is not widely recognized. It is too often assumed that if data is not directly available, then nothing can be done about it. Modelling often supplies the answer.

3.3.7 Interaction and location

We have already seen that interaction and location[30] figure significantly in social science models and especially in geography. Interaction is essentially about how many people travel from A to B for a variety of purposes.[31] The concepts are also much more general. Much of physics is based on the concept of fields – which represent interactions. Biological systems function through flows of materials, or electric pulses in the brain for instance.

Interactions, or flows, are between entities[32] at *locations* or *nodes* – origins and destinations, sources or sinks. These are representations of important parts of the structure of a system. When these ideas are built into models, they can be used to underpin performance indicators[33] and can distinguish between organizational efficiency (for instance, based on catchment populations) and effective delivery, for example.

SC 17. Interaction
SC 38. Location
SC 60. Function
SC 61. Structure
SC 62. Performance indicators
SC 63. Organizational efficiency
SC 64. Catchment populations
SC 65. Effective delivery

To fix ideas, consider again the provision of hospital treatment – the hospital system, let us call it. In a region – say, of a health authority – there will be a number of hospitals, each providing a subset of the specialisms needed for the system as a whole. They will serve people, typically, by area of residence and the residence-hospital will the basic interaction matrix. Indeed, there will be a set of such matrices, one for each specialism. In terms of the key concepts introduced in this section, therefore, the *structure* will be the spatial pattern and speciality structure of the hospitals in the area; the *functions* will be the specialist areas of treatment; the *nodes* will be the locations of the hospitals (and the centres of residential areas to be served); and the *interactions* will be flows of patients. It is intuitively obvious that it is non-trivial to find the optimum structure of such a system. From the point of view of patients, there should be hospitals nearby; from the point of view of economic provision of many specialisms, there should be a smaller number of larger hospitals. Solutions may need to be invented. For example, a compromise might be a 'hub and spoke' system, with smaller (convenient) units connected to the larger ones, so that patients can be referred on as more complex cases as appropriate. A 'flight simulator' model-based system can be used to search for optimum – or even 'good' – solutions – but, again, this is typically not done!

3.3.8 Networks

The nodes of the previous subsection are often *nodes on a network*, and the network actually 'carries' the flows. For example: traffic on a road network, current in an electrical network, nutrients in the branches of a plant. Models of flows on networks will be representations of the relevant theories or laws – Kirkhoff's laws in physics or traffic assumed to be carried on the shortest path[34] in a road network. In the latter case, the model has to be quite complicated in order to take account of congestion. In the traffic case, it is the set of flows from the interaction model that is assigned to the network and the interaction and network models can be mathematically combined.[35] Other examples included rivers, trees (figurative and literal – Woldenberg[36]) and neural networks – this last one a special case, which will be considered further below.

SC 66. Networks
SC 67. Shortest path in a network

In the last decade or so, there has been a tremendous expansion in a field that can now be described as *network science*. Interestingly, its development illustrates one of the themes of this book: it has failed to connect itself to the wider relevant research and literature and so proceeds with a less powerful engine than could be the case.[37] Those in the specialist field have focused on the topology of networks, counting the number of nodes, and the number of links connected to each node, and then finding ways of characterizing different kinds of networks. They have taken relatively little account of the flows on the links of a network and have not brought into play the elementary superconcepts of interaction and location, which would provide a way of enriching the network models.[38]

3.3.9 Complex system models: dynamics in nonlinear systems

We have now begun, through examples, to define some general concepts associated with systems – such as structure and function. We have introduced the notion of complex systems. We now show how these ideas underpin the rapidly developing field of complexity science and we can expand the argument to demonstrate the key concepts – superconcepts again – of that field. What is very important is our understanding of how systems change over time – the *dynamics of systems*. It is sometimes important to distinguish between the *fast* and the *slow* dynamics. To do this, we need the concept of *equilibrium* (which we introduced in another context – multiplicity of possible equilibria – cf. SC 26 in section 3.3.5 above). Fast dynamics refer typically to aspects of a system which, when there is a change, move to (or towards) a new equilibrium very rapidly. This is often the case for flows: water flowing in a river network, traffic on a road network, for example. Structural features – such as urban infrastructure, on the other hand, often change very slowly on a different time scale.

The key distinguishing feature of interesting complex systems is that they have nonlinear features. This means that where there is a change that generates a further change, the effect is not linear. If you depress a car accelerator at a constant rate, the response, the acceleration, will be faster than linear. In many economic processes, notwithstanding what was always taken to be a 'law of diminishing returns', there are, in fact, positive returns to scale. Supermarkets, as a food retailing sector, demonstrate this relative to 'corner shop' retailing.

Most real systems are nonlinear.[39] As size changes, there are effects which are not 'straight line' proportionate changes. Such systems have special features, some of which have only been understood in relatively recent times – and it is these features that characterize complex systems and hence are the key features of complexity science. These can be summarized as:

- multiplicity of equilibria;
- path dependence;
- significant changes – discrete changes of 'jumps' at critical points which, borrowing from physics, are sometimes termed phase transitions.

The first two of these are closely related because path dependence – dependence on 'initial conditions' – is another kind of multiplicity. The models are usually characterized by parameters – such as 'temperature' in a physical system. There may be critical values of these parameters at which abrupt changes take place – *critical points*.[40] The dependence on *initial conditions*[41] – and the combinatorial nature of possible sets of these – some of which can change as a result of, say, historical specificity – historical accidents – is at the root of the virtual impossibility of making predictions in many complex systems, even when a model is well specified. A good example is the task of weather forecasting in meteorology.

Dynamics become really interesting when the system, or aspects of the system, change in a fundamental way. This phenomenon has become known as *emergence*.[42] Examples are biological development of an organism from the combination of two cells; or, to return to an earlier example, the evolution of a retail system. The process that generates emergent properties is one of evolution.

SC 68. Fast and slow dynamics
SC 69. Equilibrium
SC 70. Nonlinear systems
SC 71. Critical points
SC 72. Initial conditions
SC 73. Emergence

We will see later that there are also versions of emergence that are analogous to phase changes in physics.[43] It is now increasingly recognized that the mechanisms used by physicists are much more widely applicable – and so this represents another superconcept, and it has been coupled with 'emergence' above in SC 21.

SC 21. Phase transitions

3.3.10   Prey–predator and competition for resources models: the origins of chaos theory

It may be helpful at this point to give another example of a nonlinear dynamical system that has applications in a variety of fields – hence giving the associated model superconcept status. This first arose in ecology as the *prey–predator model*.[44] It has been generalized in various ways as a *competition-for-resources* model.[45] It was May (1971), who in this context, showed that the simple equations of the competition-for-resources model could generate chaotic behaviour.

Let us start with the basic ecological model: there are two species – one predator, one prey. The prey population is the food for the predator population; the prey population is assumed to have a basic food supply. With plentiful supply of prey, the predator population grows steadily, but a point will be reached, where the rate of consumption of the prey is such that the prey population will become inadequate for the predator population. Not surprisingly, the usual solution to the mathematical equations that represent this system gives oscillating populations. The solution is said to be *periodic*. There has been a recent application within molecular biology by Nowak and May[46] in which viruses are competing with the antibodies of the immune system.

In the case of the competition-for-resources model, there can be several species competing for a single resource. It turns out that the same ideas can be applied in urban geography[47], chemistry[48] and politics.[49] In the urban geography case, the species are retailers (or developers of retail centres to be more precise) who are competing for consumers – their 'resource'. In chemistry, the model turns up in the physical chemistry of mixtures, where the types of molecules – the 'species' – are competing for energy. In politics, nations, for example, can be considered to be competing for resources, and Richardson based a theory of wars on the ecological model.

SC 74. Prey–predator model
SC 75. Competition-for-resources model
SC 76. Periodic solutions
SC 77. Chaos theory

3.4 Models of business and public services

3.4.1 Introduction

An important subcategory of models are those associated with business and public services. These are so different that we begin a new subsection. There are key underpinnings from economics and we begin with these in section 3.4.2 and then we turn to organizational structures[50] in section 3.4.3. These are valuable in their own right and will provide an important background to our explorations later on knowledge power – and knowledge management – in organizations.

3.4.2 Underpinning economics

Organizations, by definition, produce something – their outputs, such as cars, television sets or students with degrees. The technology – hard or soft – necessary for the production process can be represented as a *production function*: that is, the combination of materials, labour (people skills), capital and other inputs that are necessary for the processes of production – and, implicitly, an account of those processes. This means that technological change is an implicit variable in the production function.

There then is a *market* into which product can be sold at a profit; or a population of clients or consumers to whom a *service* can be delivered at a price – possibly free for some public services. All this will take place within an *environment*: the organization's supply chain, which provides access to input resources, competitors and regulation. Finally, the organization needs the appropriate *management structures and skills* – in some ways a special case of the people skills introduced above as part of the production function – but worth distinguishing because of its importance. Knowledge power must embrace all these categories. It must include the best possible understanding of past, present and future – if possible, learning from the past to have an in-house 'What if?' forecasting capability.

An understanding of the production function – and indeed, in theory, all possible alternative production functions – is a necessary condition for successful development. This means that organizations must be connected to technological knowledge – and, ideally, connected to new knowledge ahead of their competitors.

Knowledge power, therefore, involves more than can be found, typically, in the business sections of bookshops.

When the possible technologies are understood, a *strategy* is needed, and then the *means of delivery* – essentially the *management capabilities*. Together, the knowledge core, the strategy and the means of delivery constitute what, in Chapter 5, we will explore as *requisite knowledge*.

As knowledge power has become more important to organizations, it has become increasingly formally recognized. Companies often now employ chief knowledge officers and *knowledge management* has become a key concept. And, of course, within this, companies do their own R&D. Training and education has become critical in many areas and this has led to the idea of the *corporate university* – particularly in the US. However, many organizations simply have not had the capacity to create their own knowledge power, and so this period has also seen the rise of management consultants and professional training organizations. Universities have the potential, not usually realized, to fulfil all of these functions. In the way in which universities are special nodes in the knowledge system, so also are consultancies – companies that in effect have knowledge as their main product. The extent of outsourcing and partnership and alliance building will be an important strategic question.

To summarize, we have identified the knowledge needs of organizations under the headings that constitute superconcepts:

SC 78. The production 'technology'

which can have hard and/or soft elements – to generate outputs and the input resources needed to implement it, such as raw materials, land, labour and capital;

SC 79. The market (or client base)
SC 80. The business environment

whose elements might include the supply chain, competitors and systems of regulation;

SC 81. Strategy
SC 82. Delivery – management structures and skills

We need to keep in mind the sources of competitive advantage in relation to these headings. These include:

SC 83. Quality at an appropriate price

and there is a spectrum of possibilities here;

SC 84. Monopolistic benefits

through patents; location in relation to supply or markets; or regulatory privilege.

Some of these are environmental advantages that only become monopolistic if competitors can be excluded from them.

3.4.3 Models of organizations

A complementary approach to that of the economists is provided by management theorists and we can gain considerable insight from some of the models they have developed. Here we consider three – Mintzberg, Beer and Oakland.

Mintzberg's[51] is an important first-principles model. His general structure is shown in Figure 3.1.

The elements are mostly more or less self-explanatory: the upper tier of management generates the strategy; the operational units make the product or deliver the service; and there is a middle management to oversee and organize the production and delivery. There are supporting services. What he calls the 'technostructure' is about 'rules' and 'standards'. Some organizations are very routinized and rules driven; some may be less rules driven but demand very high standards. Mintzberg deduced that there were essentially five forms of organization that can be identified by seeing how the different elements of this diagram are combined in particular cases. It is useful to add these to the superconcept list.

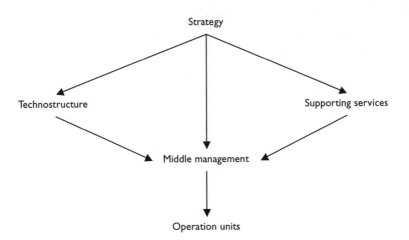

Figure 3.1 The elements of an organization.

Source: Adapted from Figure 1.2 in Mintzberg, M. (1983) *Structure in fives*, Prentice-Hall, Englewood Cliffs, NJ.

SC 85. Mintzberg's organization types
     a. simple
     b. machine
     c. professional bureaucracy
     d. divisional
     e. adhocracy

Other models have been based on analogies – and this has its own relevance to us as part of our search for superconcepts. An interesting one that has survived from the 1970s is that which originated in Stafford Beer's work in using the central nervous system as the basis of the analogy.[52] These are sometimes now known as VSMs – viable system models – perhaps an attempt to move the terminology beyond the analogy. Beer argued that the human brain is the most complex super-system to evolve in nature so that we should examine its organization to see what we can learn about effective structures. The original Beer interpretation of this structure is shown in Figure 3.2. At the upper level – level 5 – (as in Mintzberg) is 'strategy'. Level 3 is the controls of the autonomous nervous system, involving functions such as the beating heart, breathing and so on. Levels 2 and 1 involve transmission of instructions through muscles and so on – the front-line action. What is particularly interesting is level 4, which relates to information processing and especially filtering, because, Beer argues, it is missing from most organizations. He argues that the nearest equivalent is the Cabinet war room in England in World War II – and we give it superconcept status below on this basis.

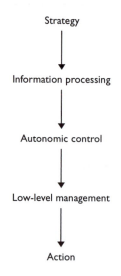

Figure 3.2 The Stafford Beer CNS/VSM model.
Source: Based on Stafford Beer (1972).

SC 86. Central nervous system (VSM) structures
SC 87. The 'war room'

It is also important to translate these insights into more straightforward business applications and this is done through the very successful *business excellence* model of Oakland.[53] The key elements are shown in Figure 3.3.

SC 88. The business excellence model

A deeper understanding of this territory will draw us into the business and management fields and we postpone any further discussion until Chapters 5, 6 and 7.

3.5 Drawing the threads together: complexity theory and systems science

In section 3.2 above, we argued that the interesting research questions were those associated with complex systems and, in subsequent sections, we have introduced, with a range of examples, a number of superconcepts whose applications cross specific systems and disciplines. A major question then is: can such concepts be put together to help formulate a *general theory of complex systems*? In short, is there such a thing as *complexity theory* or *complexity science*? We are in dangerous territory now! We noted in Chapter 2, when we first introduced the systems concept, that

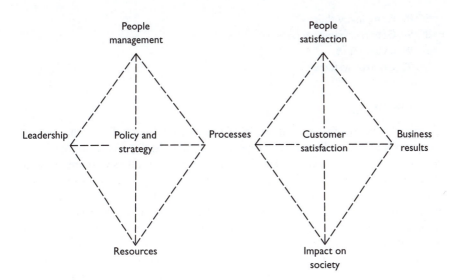

Figure 3.3 Oakland's business excellence model.

Source: Adapted from Figure 7.3 in Oakland, J. (1999) *Total organisational excellence*, Butterworth-Heinemann, Oxford.

there was an attempt in the 1950s through workers such as von Bertalanffy[54] to build a *general systems theory*. This was connected to the idea of *cybernetics* – the study of *control systems*[55] – and to an extent the work of people such as Stafford Beer[56] – note above in the context of CNS models – in operational research. There is a sense in which these enterprises all failed. No one talks about general systems theory now; cybernetics has largely come to rest in more specific territories like electrical and electronic engineering; and operational research is not the force it was in the 1960s. It would be interesting to study the sociology of these phenomena. Were they interdisciplinary fields that lost out to a reassertion of disciplinary power? Or, more likely, did they simply fail to deliver the goods?

Complexity theory had its founding locus in the Sante Fe Institute in New Mexico but is now expanding rapidly in many other places. Much of the emphasis at present is in the development of toy models of biological systems and concepts such as artificial life. However, it may be that there is a more powerful general argument to be put: that the value in the new thinking is not simply in the challenges of complexity theory, but in the recognition of the need for some fundamental shifts in scale and type at the research frontiers. There is a potential sea change from the reductionist (and microscale) to the systemic (and meso and macroscales). Some have argued that the great discoveries of the twentieth century and the completion of the human genome project, for example, proclaims the 'end of science'.[57] It might be more properly argued, with some exaggeration, that we might see the 'end of reductionism'. The big challenges are now in *systems science* and, in particular, in the development of models of systems.

SC 89. Complexity theory
SC 90. General systems theory
SC 91. Cybernetics
SC 92. Control systems

3.6 Planning

If a model is an effective one – it 'explains' the system it is modelling – then it may also provide a 'What if?' forecasting capability. Back to the flight simulator concept: no one would think of deploying a pilot without without intensive training – and with a large part of that being on a flight simulator. Suppose we had the same kind of knowledge power – because that is what training on a clever simulator is an example of – what would that be? It would be the use of models to underpin a computer simulator – a flight simulator analogue.[58] This kind of use is particularly powerful in a planning context where the consequences of a plan – of a 'design' – can be explored on a computer rather than through expensive prototypes; or in the case of cities, even more expensively on the ground. There is one note of caution to be sounded. We have shown that for nonlinear complex systems, our forecasting ability is limited. However, we can usually forecast for the short term and we can explore the consequences of future scenarios for the longer term.

In the case of cities, we could, in principle, have an accurate model-based simu-lator which predicted population growth, economic development – including job location, residential and housing development – service system development and interaction models which predicted journeys to work, shop and to use services.[59] These predictions would be dependent on certain variables being fixed – say, land-use zoning – and it is the fixing of these variables that constitutes a design. At any time, a set of performance indicators can be calculated for the city.[60] It would be a large set, but it can be done. The simulator could then be used to optimize the 'design' at any time in relation to driving chosen performance indi-cators in an appropriate direction. This is an argument that we expand at length in Chapter 4.

3.7 Computers and algorithms in modelling

3.7.1 Computer representations of systems

We have so far based our argument on conceptual shifts – towards systems analysis – and the power of mathematics in particular in facilitating the building of system models – the 'flight simulators' for a variety of systems. The third dimension of the argument is based on the rapid development of computer technology. What is now possible takes us beyond – or enhances – information systems and data-bases. Systems and system models are represented on computers, and our ability to cope with big systems is totally dependent on computer power. In traditional mathematics, simple systems could be understood analytically in, say, algebraic terms: equations could be 'solved'. For big systems, it is now commonplace to recognize that computers are needed to solve the equations and indeed to facil-itate the *visualization* of the solutions. In this way, there is a critical interaction between computer power and mind power – and through this interaction we can recognize another dimension of knowledge power.

SC 93. Computer models
SC 94. Computer visualization

In an earlier section (3.2), we noted the importance of explicitly articulating the system of interest. Such explicitness is forced on us in building a computer system or model: we have to specify how each element, and the interactions, are to be represented. There are choices, for example, according to scale. To represent a city in a model – as discussed in the preceding section – do we use individuals in the population, or groups of individuals? In this case, it can be done either way. To represent an urban transport system, for example, the city can be divided into discrete zones, and the transport pattern represented by the number of people travelling from any zone to any other zone. People are combined into trip bun-dles – a kind of mesolevel representation. Alternatively, we can list all the people in the city – as a hypothetical population that has the same properties as a real population – and assign an origin-destination pair of addresses to each 'person'. This is a microlevel representation. In the mesolevel representation, if the city is divided into 100 zones, then the trip pattern would be represented by a 100×100 matrix (which would have 10,000 elements). In the microlevel one, there may be a million people to list. The resulting models are known as microsimulation models.[61] With modern computing power either representation is possible. The choice must fit both purpose and feasibility. As computers become more powerful, the first of these can predominate.

SC 95. Microsimulation

We should also note the impact of Web 2.0 technology in relation to this kind of computer modelling. Web 2.0 is essentially about collaboration. There are a number of implications of this. Researchers can share software and data and can work in virtual teams. The models can be shared with a wider community thus widening participation in various planning processes.

3.7.2 Algorithms

The two most distinctive features of powerful computers are memory size and processing speed. At an elementary level, computers can be thought of as storing and manipulating large databases. The manipulation will include, for example, arithmetic. This simple idea is illustrated by the spreadsheet, which will be familiar to most readers. When mathematical models have to be represented and, for example, algebraic equations have to be solved, computers deploy algorithms.[62,63] Algorithmic thinking can be different from conventional mathematics and in later chapters we will provide examples.[64]

Computer manipulations and algorithms represented in computer programmes and large programmes can only be written with great skill and at substantial cost. This has led computer scientists to work at higher levels of generality than the specific task in hand and to develop languages so that code that is developed for one task or problem can be used for another. This is illustrated by the concept of object-oriented programming. It is particularly interesting in the context of this book that there is a direct and not always clearly stated connection to systems analysis: the objects, often in a hierarchical structure, are the elements of (general) systems. Because the systems are large, these can be computer representations of complex systems. A related approach is that of OLAP systems[65] - online analytical process systems.

SC 96. Computer algorithms
SC 97. Graphical models

3.7.3 Intelligent search

In concentrating on algorithms in the previous subsection, the emphasis was on processing. Expanding memory capacities have made computers huge stores of data and information – numerical and text. The exploration of planning scenarios using 'flight simulator' models can be recorded as information – now perhaps better described as 'intelligence' – within a computer system. This has put emphasis on such concepts as data warehousing and data mining.[66] To make sense of these mounds of information and intelligence, there is a first concern with classification issues and then above all with search problems and navigation. One long-standing approach to all these issues has been through artificial intelligence (AI) – but some now argue that the promise has not been delivered and that it will turn out to be a wrong road (cf. Holland[67]).

SC 98. Intelligent search

However, this will remain a critical concept, not least because of the achievements of companies such as Google and Yahoo in developing extraordinary search engines. But much of the intelligence has to be added by the user! This adds to the argument earlier about Web 2.0 and collaboration through the internet. This is reinforced by the wiki-culture.[68] Wikipedia is impressive and is now universally used – but the idea of different uses of wiki software for more targeted team work, in education or for building individual knowledge resource systems is as yet underdeveloped.

3.7.4 Neural networks and pattern recognition

Notwithstanding the comment about AI above, one particular approach is worth particular notice – that of deploying the concept of *neural networks*.[69] As the name implies, the technique involves mimicking neural structures in the brain. At one level, neural network algorithms also mimic what might be called a *statistical machine* and it remains an interesting research problem to prove all the equivalences.[70] One recurring problem that fits this bill is that of pattern recognition. As the underlying concept implies, neural models can be learning models – another interesting computer challenge.[71] Such models can, in principle, also be *adaptive*. Finally, we note computers as cellular automata.[72]

SC 99. Neural networks
SC 100. Adaptive systems

3.8 Knowledge systems

In summary, the path we are charting is to move beyond data and information systems to intelligence – to *knowledge systems*. We need clever navigation systems that can turn information systems into *intelligent* information systems.[73] This all connects to the currently fashionable concept of knowledge management.[74] We have argued that knowledge is about understanding, and appropriate understanding for the contemporary age can only be achieved through a combination of breadth and depth, and this means interdisciplinarity. The depth of understanding achieved in the highest levels of the traditional disciplines will remain crucial, but there will be huge scope for developing new kinds of courses. As we will see, interdisciplinarity is already evident in research but has, as yet, had much less impact on the teaching curriculum.

The analysis of this chapter begins to provide a framework for new ways of thinking. We now need to show how these new ways might be deployed, first in terms of knowledge development in Chapter 4 and then in terms of its impact on organizations, communities and individuals in subsequent chapters.

Chapter 4

Knowledge development

How will the knowledge base, whether through disciplines or interdisciplinary frameworks, develop in the future? Provisional answers to this question will guide us to new priorities for future development – in education and more widely.

4.1 Introduction

We have now structured the knowledge base in terms of disciplines and interdisciplinary areas (Chapter 2); and we have identified some major shifts in the approach to knowledge in the future – the systems and models foci and the deployment of superconcepts (Chapter 3). We can now combine these two sets of foundations and begin to explore substantively what the shifts are likely to be in particular fields – and indeed, in some cases, what the shifts *ought* to be.

There are two critical issues: can the big problems, as we now understand them – the superproblems – be tackled in new ways? Are there new problems, or new application areas, using existing concepts and superconcepts to be tackled in new ways?

With these questions in mind, we start with a review of disciplines – using the structure of Chapter 2, but ordered slightly differently. Then we move on to interdisciplinary priorities. However, it will be evident in the 'discipline' sections that it is impossible to discuss the biggest problems without setting the agenda for interdisciplinary approaches.

4.2 The abstract and enabling disciplines

We begin with a brief review of some potential shifts in the key enabling disciplines,[1] focusing on mathematics and computer science. Mathematics can revolutionize many disciplines. But for this to be achieved, the fundamental stance of at least some mathematicians has to change. First, some background.

In mathematics, there has been a long tradition of integrating – seeing as equivalent – what might originally be seen as distinct fields. An obvious historical example that we noted earlier is provided by geometry and algebra – the link provided by the invention of the (Cartesian in the first place) coordinate system and algebraic geometry. This has had its most dramatic manifestation in recent times with Andrew Wiles' proof of Fermat's last theorem[2], which relied on integration of ideas from otherwise unconnected branches of pure mathematics. It is also established that pure mathematicians, working in an abstract world, often find that their research does have applications many years later – indeed, often beyond the lifetimes of the creators. However, it is perhaps a characteristic of the modern world that the time span from pure invention to practical application is shortening. Rene Thom's development of catastrophe theory, published in the early 1970s, had a dramatic and rapid effect, for example, on the development of techniques in applied mathematics, which facilitated the development of models of nonlinear systems.[3]

However, this example also illustrates a critical defect in the practice of applied mathematics. There is a tendency for applied mathematicians to develop such ideas in the context of a rather idealized form of application – in a sense to mimic the work of the pure mathematicians – to 'finish it off'! Much of the work of applying mathematics is actually done by practitioners in other disciplines, such as theoretical physicists, engineers or economists. The suspicion then is that the applied mathematicians consider such work 'routine' because it is not developing the mathematics. However, this view has two consequences. First, the most powerful mathematicians do not work on the most important applied problems; and second, the applied mathematicians do not open themselves rapidly enough, or indeed at all, to the challenging mathematical problems thrown up in other disciplines. In particular, in terms of one of the core arguments of this book, they do not open themselves up to *big system* problems. They are too often content to work with idealized 'toy' models with techniques that do not lend themselves to scaling up. All this leaves obvious opportunities for new developments. If these attitudes can be changed, then a revolution becomes possible. *The key to the revolution is building mathematical models of complex systems.* We will see many examples of this in subsequent sections. And, of course, our ability to make progress in this direction also turns on computer science, the second key enabling discipline and it is to this that we now turn.

In some ways, the rate of progress in computer science seems to have been more rapid than that in applied mathematics.[4] Computing has certainly revolutionized work in all disciplines. But there are opportunities for development of a similar kind to those in applied mathematics, which would accelerate the revolution, but arise for different reasons. The advances in computer science have been driven from the hardware technology side – mainly memory and processing power, but also in terms of convenience of use – and from the software side through the development of more powerful languages and applications, including databases, search systems and visualization capabilities. (Many of the applications are commercially oriented, and we pick this up in our discussion of business below.) We have also already seen that there has been a drive towards higher levels of generality with the development of concepts such as *object-oriented programming,* which is very much a form of systems analysis. Because this is technologically driven from within the discipline, there has been relatively little interdisciplinary work, though this is beginning to change with the development of fields such as informatics.[5]

There is another major pointer to future change, led by computer science: the increase in both memory and processing capacity has facilitated the assembly of huge databases. This has an impact in most disciplines, but perhaps particularly, for the future, in the social sciences. There is now a massive amount of data collected on human behaviour – by retailers, banks and credit card companies, for example. Wireless and satellite technologies – in mobile phones, for instance – now means that movements of individuals can be charted. Most of this data is as yet unused, and its use does, of course, raise privacy issues. This technology is the basis of a surveillance society: movements tracked, behaviour monitored on CCTV (with the possibility of face recognition software being used to assign identities to CCTV images). Genetic data on individuals can be used in health care but also, potentially, by the insurance industry.

As we have already seen in a number of contexts, there has been relatively little model-based work – building the analogues of the flight simulator in a variety of fields. There are major opportunities, therefore, for interdisciplinary developments in which the best mathematicians and computer scientists are fully integrated in teams working on complex system modelling. Again, a major shift is needed. However, given the cultural foundations of disciplines, this will not be easy to achieve. We will give substantive examples in various subsections below.

4.3 The core physical sciences: the basis of technological development

What can we say about the future of physics? And what can we learn for other fields? The lure of the fundamental is irresistible at both micro- and macroscales. A small number of highly talented physicists will always work in these areas, and students will always want to engage with them. (It is no accident that many Physics Departments now characterize themselves as Departments of Physics and Astronomy!) There are major theoretical problems: quantum mechanics at the Planck limit; and perhaps above all, the possibility of a 'theory of everything' that integrates quantum mechanics, gravity and relativity theory.[6] There are remarkable advances in cosmology, both observationally and theoretically.[7] There will be interesting spin-offs from these areas: quantum computing and the possibility of applying the mathematics of high dimensional spaces – as in string theory – in other disciplines. But perhaps the bulk of effort will go into the difficult challenges of fields of potential application – in electronics and the world of solid-state devices; communications technologies in areas such as opto-electronics; new imaging devices with applications in medicine; polymers and materials science; the application of the enormous levels of skill now available in areas such as fluid dynamics. Many of these are complex systems problems.

Some fundamental shifts are now becoming clear. In polymer physics, for example, the methods for determining the properties of particular polymers were essentially experimental. It is now becoming possible to build explicit mathematical models of polymer structures and to determine properties from these. This opens up the possibilities of designing polymers with desirable properties on computers and then creating them physically. This is a good example of a field that will be revolutionized by mathematical-computer modelling. And since proteins are essentially polymers, these techniques can be developed in collaboration with molecular biologists and the pharmaceuticals industry – giving biophysics a new life.

All of these areas will connect strongly to different branches of engineering – particularly to rapidly developing areas like nanotechnology. As the manipulation of smaller and smaller units becomes technically feasible – even individual atoms and electrons – this begins to define the ground for new computing technologies, and in particular quantum, optical (holographic) and neural net computers.[8]

Physicists have worked in biology since the early days of X-ray crystallography. In the post-genome age, biologists will work increasingly in fields like proteonomics, and in particular, protein folding. Proteins, as we noted earlier, are polymers and there is much scope for the sharing of skills. Chemists also have a long history of working in biology, and indeed what started as an interdisciplinary subject – biochemistry – has now become one of the key disciplines of molecular biology.

What are the possibilities of shifts to a systems focus? Much of physics is directed towards small (and in some cases idealized) systems. There are possibilities of extending the methods of statistical mechanics as they have been applied to solids – for example, building on Ising models[9], particularly in the modelling of phase transitions. It is interesting that this kind of mathematical physics is now being presented as a more generally applicable set of concepts that extend beyond physics – mirroring our notion of superconcepts.[10] The idea of quantum computing can perhaps be thought of as an interesting scale shift!

Similar arguments can be applied to chemistry as a discipline: it can be seen as the physics of big molecules and their interactions. There are big systems which demand combinations of skills: atmospheric chemistry in relation to problems of pollution and climate change, for example, which demands linking fluid dynamics to the physics and chemistry of atmospheric gases. This is another area where there are huge mathematical and computer modelling challenges. And, as with physics, as biologists become ever more successful at the microscale, the skills of the chemists can be added to, for example, in structural biology teams.

On an even bigger scale, all of these skills combine in the discipline of meteorology and the development of models that underpin weather forecasting. This begins to link us to the broader range of issues of earth and environmental sciences. There are certainly some big systems' problems and universities find it very difficult to cope with these kinds of systems because of their interdisciplinary nature. Those agencies who could, like government departments, do not manage to do so effectively either. A research council, like the NERC[11], does better. However, environmental issues are a mixture of the physical, the biological and the social and so we develop the argument progressively through the following subsections and then rejoin in a full interdisciplinary context in section 4.9.

There are big systems problems also in the socio-economic-geographic sciences at the scales of cities, regions and nations[12] and we note here that some of these can be tackled using superconcepts from the core sciences, like entropy[13], but we defer these until section 4.7 below.

4.4 Living systems: biology and medicine

There are certainly major unsolved problems and issues with big systems: the brain, many diseases, problems of diagnosis, evidence-based medicine – connecting research to practice under the heading of health services research – all provide examples. But we should start with the area that has dominated the biological sciences since Crick and Watson published their account of the structure of DNA in 1953[14] – molecular biology. This is the triumph of reductionist science. DNA – the genetic code – represents the mechanism by which biological material can replicate, in Crick's own words, the basis of 'life itself'.[15] It provides the template not only for reproducing itself, but for generating RNA and the proteins which form the basis of our physiology. It is the study of the 'behaviour' of these proteins – in areas such as protein folding – that determines how our bodies function, and whether they function normally or not. Hence, of course, the direct link between post-genomic science and medicine.

A primary research task lasting over half a century has been that of articulating the full genetic code, now formally completed. This represents a staggering achievement. And, as we have indicated, molecular biologists will progress towards new depths. However, there are also opportunities at this scale to add conceptual power. Consider the new subdiscipline of bioinformatics. It should be concerned with modelling and systems analysis, but is focused mainly on the manipulation and visualization of large data sets and on statistical analysis. The new opportunity in the post-genomic age is in functional biology – the study of the proteins produced on genetic templates and their roles. Much is already known about protein structures from the long-standing but still advancing field of crystallography. However, future interest will be in the ways in which proteins can fold themselves and play different biological roles in different folded states. Then, to quote Kaku, referring to protein folding:

> When a protein cannot be crystallised, one cannot use X-ray crystallography to determine its structure. Scientists are forced to use the quantum theory and electrostatics to find the structure of the protein. The complex equations which determine the structure of these proteins can only be solved by using computers ... [which] may be the only way to calculate the structure and hence the properties of a large class of proteins.[16]

This is the biological equivalent of the polymer modelling example cited in the previous section. It is another powerful illustration of the potential revolutionary impact of mathematical-computer modelling of complex systems.

It goes without saying that this research will underpin an expanding biotechnology industry. One of the challenges in finding effective new drugs is to identify biological sites – which may be folded proteins to continue with the theme of this example. At present, much of this work has to be done experimentally in the laboratory. A new model-based bioinformatics would enable this to be done by computer, in effect using the modelled interactions for making 'What if?' predictions. This will begin to reshape the very expensive research enterprises in large pharmaceutical companies. At present, candidate drugs can be generated using the machinery of combinatorial chemistry and their biological interactions explored in the laboratory. Since thousands of candidates can be produced in a very short time, this is a massive labour-consuming and expensive effort. How much of this can be done using computer models? In the future, the answer to this question is likely to be: quite a lot!

There will also be opportunities for scale shifts in biology – particularly to confront the new big system problems at scales larger than the genome or the protein. Such problems of complexity, of the 'new' physiology, are sometimes embraced under the title *integrative* or *systems* biology. The adjectives are appropriate: the shift of scale to a systemic level forces integration, takes us beyond increasing specialism and compartmentalism. In medicine, for example, it creates a perspective through which it becomes possible to link more effectively general practice and medical specialisms through a patient focus – something that is sadly lacking at the present time. (As noted earlier, 'diagnosis' is essentially a systemic task.) This can be seen as 'physiology' rising again in importance as a subdiscipline relative to molecular biology.

The scales range from the molecular via the cell and the organism to the ecosystem. Theory at all scales remains underpinned in many respects by Darwin's concept of evolution – the principle of which is often described as the 'survival of the fittest'. What remains a big issue is to understand in detail the *mechanisms* of evolution. There is one view that adaptation in more successful species is not fast enough to explain the rate at which more advanced species have developed. It remains, however, a powerful concept, and certainly a superconcept that has in this case been picked up in a wide variety of fields. To 'evolution' as a key concept, we should add from contemporary complexity theory that of 'emergence'. How do new structures develop and emerge from and within systems in such surprising ways? How does a human being emerge from the conjunction of two cells? This, as we noted earlier, is the classical problem of developmental biology. Much is known, but the theory is still hugely incomplete.[17] And we should observe that these ideas can be carried through into many other disciplines. How cities evolve over time is a question analogous to those of developmental biology.

An underlying principle of evolution is that of *competition* and this provides a metaphor for other systems. In ecosystems, for example, there are two fundamental models – introduced in Chapter 3 – which have been developed as mathematical models since the 1920s: the prey–predator model and the competition-for-resources model.[18] Even simpler models, for example that of logistic growth in the work of Robert May have been shown to incorporate complex dynamical behaviour – and, as we saw in Chapter 3, presaged aspects of complexity theory.[19] These ideas have re-emerged from a different perspective in urban geography, as we will see in section 4.6 below.

We have already given some indication of the implications of biological research for medicine. This is an appropriate point to summarize and extend that discussion. We have predicted the consequences of a more advanced form of bioinformatics on the pharmaceutical industry – the possibility of designing more effective drugs for a variety of purposes. And we have mentioned some potential organizational advances associated with diagnosis. But the changes to come are more fundamental than these.[20] It is anticipated that a high proportion of human disease is grounded in genetics; and hence the decoding of the human genome will enable much earlier diagnosis of potential medical problems for each individual. (And, of course, there are obvious implications, as noted in the computer science context above, for industries such as insurance.) It will become increasingly possible to tackle these problems at the molecular level – so that molecular medicine and gene therapies will command a greater part of medicine.

4.5 Design and invention: engineering

Engineering is about the exploitation of science for specific ends, though engineers, especially in universities, often practice as scientists, while scientists – for example, in the design of equipment – often work like engineers![21] The engineer's task is to *design* devices and machines, and, if what is needed does not exist, to *invent*.[22] The skills of design and invention are fundamentally different to the analytical skills of the scientist. In fact, this is a convenient point to emphasize a superconcept trio. There is a third type of thinking: the articulation of *policy*. Thus, to tackle a problem, there are usually three elements: articulating policy (setting objectives), design (invention) and analysis.[23]

SC 35. Policy, design and analysis: three ways of thinking

Engineering cannot be characterized in a simple way. It is practised and perceived in different ways in different kinds of organizations. In universities, emphasis is given to the scientific base, and in one sense the acquiring of this knowledge is proper because this is a necessary condition to be satisfied by a qualified engineer. Industry, however, wants practitioners who can work in an integrated way – typically on big systems such as an aircraft. The picture is then further complicated by the influence of the big engineering institutions such as The Institution of Mechanical Engineers. The Victorian structure of these controllers of the engineering professions – symbolized in London by their Great George Street and Birdcage Walk buildings – causes an unattractive degree of compartmentalism if the need is for *systems* engineers.

What are the superproblems and issues? We have already noted the need for scale shifts – particularly to big 'systems'. There is also a reverse trend as developments in electronics accelerate – to miniaturization – which ultimately takes us into areas such as quantum computing – engineering at the Planck limit. This is the field of nanotechnology. Engineering also increasingly connects to biology and medicine on the one hand – a major new interdisciplinary interface in areas such as tissue engineering – and in biotechnology, a major addition to chemical engineering within the field of process engineering. Other shifts are brought about through the impact of IT and the convergence of electronic technologies. The former means that engineering is now as much concerned with 'soft' technologies as with 'hard'. And the fields of telecommunications, computing and media are converging and creating new challenges and opportunities for engineers.

Where do the conceptual shifts come from? Engineers have always been good mathematicians and are well placed to take advantage of the explicit mathematical and computer modelling of materials discussed earlier. This will be particularly important in fields like materials engineering where there is now the possibility of designing (smart) materials. They have also always been good practitioners of mathematical modelling in macro fields such as transport engineering and they will be well placed to expand these roles as a member of multidisciplinary 'urban systems' teams.

Perhaps above all, engineering needs to break down the barriers posed by the professional institutions whose boundaries are underpinned by an older science: civil, mechanical, electrical and electronic, chemical and a number of more specialized areas such as textiles. The main problems are now process and systems problems and a focus on systems engineering is likely to be more productive.

4.6 The social sciences

The social sciences are often seen as 'soft' and the poor relations of the 'hard' sciences. They are indeed poor relations in terms of funding, but it is evident that some of the biggest problems and issues reside in this territory as we saw in Chapter 2. There is a need to understand economic transformation – globally, nationally, regionally and locally. This implies understanding the geography: cities, regions and nations; and, for example, the contemporary patterns of population migration. The economic transformation has huge social consequences. Both globally and locally, there is an increasing gap between rich and poor. This social exclusion exacerbates the problems of drugs and crime. There is a huge *education* challenge. And, of course, social science is, in general, more directly connected to public policy issues than the other sciences. The notion of evidence-based medicine has now been translated into the broader arena of evidence-based policy, both in government and in the Economic and Social Research Council.

In physics, we reviewed the fundamentals of the science at different scales. In the social sciences, the subject has become compartmentalized into different disciplines – in part for understandable reasons, but in such a way that it is now very difficult to assemble an integrated assessment of the progress in understanding that has been achieved. This partly arises because of a fundamental issue in the social sciences – the agency-structure problem. It is possible to focus on an individual within a social structure – in the broadest sense, his or her environment. This is fundamentally the subject matter of psychology, but also of micro-economics and parts of social geography. The key problem at a bigger scale is: how does the social structure *emerge*? To what extent can any one individual influence or change it? That is the agency-structure problem. It is a key task of the social sciences to confront this. In practice, what is more likely to happen is that assumptions or approximations will be made by theorists to enable progress to be made.

The core disciplines which make up the social sciences have initially emerged from particular perspectives: psychology on the individual and the mind; sociology on the individual in society and social structures; economics on consumer and organizational behaviour; and human geography on place. Business schools have taken management and organizations as interdisciplinary foci – mainly by concentrating on companies, and to a lesser extent, public sector organizations. Each discipline has evolved theories to embrace their own territories, but there has been little attempt to integrate across the social sciences. There are some signs of change: some economists are viewing the economy as a complex system[24,25,26] (including a preparedness to weaken some of the classic assumptions, such as diminishing returns to scale and to recognize positive returns in some circumstances). There are related new approaches – such as those of evolutionary economics.[27] And there is a return to the skills of cost–benefit analysis.[28] Geographers, more than other disciplines, have taken cities and regions as foci. Business schools have faced up to the challenges of e-commerce. This last case illustrates a dramatic interaction between computing and communications developments and business – in particular, through the impact of the internet. This, in effect, has generated a completely new mode of production. Manufacturers of consumer goods can now sell through the internet (though most still have the physical problem of delivery). The conventional retailer, in some instances, could disappear.[29] This situation demands new economic and business models – analogous to the introduction of new transport modes.[30] This illustrates the impact of an essentially simple idea that demands immensely complicated technology to deliver. Thinking about new 'modes' also has implications for new and much-needed methods of public service delivery and we pursue these in Chapter 5. (These issues raise questions of marketing channels and such like and connect back to the sections in Chapter 3 on interaction and networks.)

Part of the theoretical challenge is, as usual, to bring about scale shifts – particularly to systems foci, and to take on the task of relating micro-, macro- and mesoscales. In this context, some new representations of systems are becoming important, particularly microsimulation.[31,32] Above all, what is needed is the capability to add conceptual power through the integration of the core disciplines. This would facilitate the development of new application areas, for example, in health, education and other areas of social analysis.

What we have seen is a set of disciplines whose history has brought about a structure determined by approach rather than by system. There have been some shifts, such as specialist institutes, which focus in a specialist way on such topics as transport and health. What no one has succeeded in doing is to focus on the big systems, such as cities and regions, the understanding of which demands an integration of all the social science disciplines (and more).[33] There is, therefore, a massive theoretical challenge to be undertaken, that is the integration of the theory of the social sciences – integrative social science – an analogue of integrative biology – but in this case, there is a much bigger challenge because of the disconnected conceptual bases of the elements.

4.7 Action: politics and management

4.7.1 Towards intelligent information systems

Because the social sciences are nearer to social action, there is a close link between the two. Economic policy, for example, does typically flow from economic analysis. But this is also an appropriate place to point out a critical distinction between the physical and biological sciences and the social sciences: when it comes to action, there is not necessarily any agreement on the way forward. Hence real politics! (And these disagreements are sometimes reflected in the underlying science.)[34] There are areas, perhaps in management or operational research, where action can easily be agreed, but where different views on values are involved, whether as in the traditional left versus right or on alternative dimensions. The Habermas 'consensus theory of truth' argument presented in Chapter 2 is relevant here: the 'science' – the technical elements – is what can easily be agreed on; the 'politics' is not, in this sense, a science, though social science can still be used to explore the consequences of the options.

The fundamental value questions turn up through the disciplines of politics (as well as its public practice). The big questions are well rehearsed. If we are seeking to optimize something, what should the 'something' be? The ethical issues are not capable of any agreement, although philosophers have worked hard over the centuries to state some basic principles that might provide a core. The utilitarian principle[35] and the categorical imperative[36] are two of the most important.

Economic policy can be based on models of economies: the *input–output*[37] model is a particularly significant one. Geography can offer performance indicators[38] to represent markets, catchments and competition. Management can represent what Mintzberg calls types of bureaucracy as we saw in Chapter 3.[39] There is a miasma of management theories, often apparently individualized to promote a particular author. Rather than try to find a general theory in this area it is perhaps better to think of a tool kit.[40]

This area is so important to everyday lives and yet so inadequately researched, that it is worth developing in more detail. Take the UK as an example. City regions embrace most of the population and provide an interesting focus for seeking to understand government issues and search for solutions. Knowledge power is about 'understanding' and 'problem-solving', so what can it offer – as the social science of action – cities and local and national governments? The answer is: a huge amount, the bases of evidence-based policy.

Government policy on the big issues is almost always formulated on a national basis as though there is a single prescription to tackle issues that in practice manifest themselves in different ways locally. In our terms, this is macro (or occasionally micro), when what is needed is meso. By adopting a 'town, city and region' perspective, policies can be tested nearer to their point of impact and the knowledge gained can be fed back. Different policies may be needed for towns, cities and conurbations of different shapes and sizes. It also very quickly becomes clear that joined-up government is essential – a kind of interdisciplinarity.

Consider in turn two perspectives: a city in aggregate within a system of cities; and a finer-scale view of a particular city and its neighbourhoods. A city can be characterized by its economy on the one hand and its population on the other. What is its role in the national economy? How is it competing with other cities? Does it offer an adequate range of jobs for its population? Does it have good economic development policies? Is it prosperous? If not, at what rate could it be developed or regenerated? Is it well connected through transport and telecommunications to the rest of the country, or indeed, the world? Is the population stable or shifting in some way? How does it locate itself within the patterns of international migration? Is it sufficiently skilled to enable it to compete?

Within a city, does the housing supply meet the needs of the population? Is there good access to appropriate employment? Is the population well served in terms of major public services such as health and education? Do people feel safe and enjoy a good environment? Are the elderly well provided for?

Scarcely a central government department in the UK is untouched by these kinds of questions. Various sectors and their departments can be seen as follows:

- Economy – The Treasury (HMT), Business, Innovation and Skills (BIS) and Work and Pensions (DWP);
- Migration – Children, Schools and Families (DCSF), DWP and the Home Office;
- Education – schools and universities (DCSF and BIS);
- Health – hospitals and health centres (DH);
- Culture – Culture, Media and Sport (DCMS);
- Safety – Home Office and Justice;
- Transport – DoT;
- Food and environment –DEFRA;
- Recruitment to public services – DH, DCSF, Defence (MoD);
- Housing and planning – Communities and Local Government (CLG).

All of these departments will preach the mantra of 'evidence-based' policy. The same argument can be put for local government.

Too often, questions are formulated as single issues rather than through a systems perspective, e.g. should there be a third runway at Heathrow? The pros and cons are then evaluated on a very narrow basis. Any one question can usually be broken down into three. What are we trying to achieve? How can we achieve it? How can we analyse the context and evaluate alternative schemes? (The alternatives always include 'do nothing'.) It is usually necessary to generate provisional answers to these questions and then to iterate – to complete the cycle again, deepening knowledge and understanding each time. These can be summarized as policy, design (or invention) and analysis. In the Heathrow runway case, the policy questions immediately broaden: how can we cope with the anticipated demand for air travel? The associated analysis question is: how can we predict this demand? The design question in this case is: what are the alternatives? Expand Luton or Stansted? Build a new airport in the Thames Gateway? Restrict air travel? The evaluation part of the analysis then involves a full account of all the costs and benefits. The methodologies for these studies exist, but they are not being systematically applied.

The full range of social sciences has something to offer – but I will concentrate on territories within my own experience and the superconcepts of Chapter 3: the analysis of geographical information on cities and city regions and the deployment of that information in planning and problem-solving. The most advanced form of that analysis is represented in mathematical and computer models, which, in appropriate circumstances, offer a 'What if?' forecasting capability: 'flight simulators' for evidence-based policy building. This kind of analytical capability has been available for four decades or more but has only been applied in the public sector on a very limited basis, though it has been extensively used in the private sector. There have probably been two main reasons for this: lack of quantitative social scientists to fully sustain the research programme, and, partly associated with this and partly with the amateur generalist traditions of the British Civil Service, a lack of appreciation in government of what can be achieved. The situation could be about to change: first, because the problems are so acute that this may create fertile territory for a new approach; and second, because the availability of data and computing power make the analysis cheaper and therefore more feasible – and, indeed, potentially more powerful. There is still a need for more skilled practitioners, however.

As we have seen, economists routinely build input–output models of national economies and, to a more limited extent, of regional economies. It would be valuable to apply these methods to urban economies. This would facilitate an assessment of likely and feasible paths of economic development, the extent to which market forces will deliver a good outcome and whether certain kinds of infrastructure investment would bring about a sea change in areas of deprivation. There are new insights to be developed and captured at the city and regional scales. We are familiar, through national input–output models, of the importance of a positive balance of payments for the future of an economy. The same applies at the more local scales even though this is not usually measured, and this kind of knowledge should be part of the development of city and regional economic strategies. In areas where regeneration is the key issue, this immediately exposes the connectivity of the issues: education, transport, health, social security and crime. Demographers can build good population forecasting models that under-pin estimates of demand for public services from school places to care needs of the elderly. However, these forecasts are not robust against major migration flows and they need to be monitored separately.

There are good and effective computer models for estimating transport flows – whether at the inter-urban or intra-urban scales. These can be used for evaluating transport infrastructure projects, congestion charging and road pricing, or for air-port policy. They can also tell us who is likely to use each facility within a system: schools and hospitals, to take two obvious examples. In either of these cases, the models could be used to evaluate the government's 'choice' agenda. It is possible to calculate performance indicators of two kinds: the first kind is commonly used – referring to institutions such as schools and hospitals and leading to the whole apparatus of league tables; the second is less obvious, and is not the same – measur-ing the effectiveness of delivery to a segment of population at a location.

There is a relatively recent development that is important for the argument that follows: it is now possible to construct a hypothetical population of a city with detailed characteristics which closely mimic the real population. This technique is known as *microsimulation* and has a number of advantages. With the help of com-puter models, it can generate the population on the basis of *sample* data. This is very important since it is often argued that it is lack of data that inhibits the kinds of development proposed here. Second, it is possible to work at a very fine scale without infringing the Data Protection Act, since this 'population' is realistic but hypothetical. The whole analysis system of the kind described here would provide a basis for more effective city and regional planning.

If this knowledge base was applied systematically in a city, the outputs could be stored in a vast (in computer storage terms) information warehouse. This would include all the raw data, or links to access the data on other servers, as well as the results of model-based analyses and of particular projects. At the lowest level, there would be very fine categorizations of people and organizations, and then there would be various aggregations for different purposes. There is clever software now available – wikis, for example – to structure such a system to make search and access relatively straightforward. It is easy to build user-friendly front-ends, for example using a touch-table geographical information system – an equivalent of the old Cabinet Office 'War Room', this time for city planning and government. It could perhaps be called a 'City Intelligence System' – a CIS. There could also be a central government version of this available too – a GovIS? – which would provide both a common information base across departments, and a bespoke ele-ment for individual departments.

It is unlikely that a good City Intelligence System exists anywhere in the world. In the UK, there is extensive use of transport models but relatively few other model-based analyses. There is a potentially supportive research base in the universities – much of it supported by the Economic and Social Research Council – but on a relatively small scale and not strongly connected to practice. There are extensive research programmes in government departments, but these tend to be relatively short-term statistical evaluations of policies. There is little that contributes to CIS or GovIS development. In spite of the mantras of 'joined-up government', much of the work, locally and centrally, is carried out in silos. Also, in the civil service, the analytical services are finely divided into professions – economics, statistics, social, operational research, science and so on – and this does not encourage an integrated approach to intelligence for planning and problem-solving. This means that projects are not analysed on a joined-up basis – that is, looking beyond their immediate consequences; alternatives are not systematically explored; full cost–benefit analyses are not carried out. What are the future possibilities? We begin by reviewing areas that are the responsibility of one or two departments and then move on to the interconnectedness agenda.

4.7.2 Economic development

There is a Public sector agreement (PSA) target, probably now jointly owned by the Treasury and [Department of] Business, Innovation and Skills (BIS), that relates to the equalization of GDP per capita across English regions. This may be politically laudable, but its feasibility should be tested through some economic modelling. There are some major hypotheses to test. For example, will the maximum rate of growth of the UK economy be achieved if London and the South East are encouraged to maximize their growth, possibly at the expense of that PSA target? And if we examine regional targets, what are the bases for achieving them? To begin with, the big cities are typically the engines of regional growth. How much does improvement in GDP per capita in a region depend on improving GDP in problem areas such as inner cities? What is the ongoing economic function of small towns in a region – for example, seaside towns, often with fine architecture, but run down and without an adequate range of good job opportunities, and therefore, income?

The core policy, whether for cities or regions, is clear: maximize economic growth. It is much less clear whether there is, in different locations, a systematic study of alternatives. Is a casino the only possibility to underpin regeneration in places such as Blackpool or East Manchester? And, of course, there are strong connections to education, health, culture and environment which we will pick up later.

4.7.3 Migration

Data on migration is very poor. Some local authorities face new pressures from concentrations of new migrants from Eastern Europe, for example. If the issues could be adequately charted, there could be a more effective government response. It is often felt that these kinds of questions can only be tackled with 100 per cent data, usually only achieved at 10-year censuses. However, this is an example of where the 160 or so local authorities in England, led by the Home Office, could be asked to undertake sample surveys which could almost certainly build up a better and more systematic picture relatively quickly. Policy development, exploration of a range of responses and effective analysis could then follow.

4.7.4 Education

Data on pupils and schools is beginning to be very good, but is not yet wholly connected. In principle it should be possible to track individual performance through the education system and be in a position to take action when 'failure' of some kind is identified. Much progress has been made on measuring a school's performance. There is more controversy on what to do about 'failing' schools, and indeed on basic geography: is there an optimum size for different kinds of schools, for example, in relation to the average travel-to-school distances that different patterns would generate? If head teachers are critical – and the population of good ones is too low – can appropriate federations of schools be assembled? If the process of improvement is to be driven by parental choice, how can we measure the adequacy of 'choice' that is on offer? This last question is one that could be tackled analytically but this has not been done – unless there are local instances.

University admissions are also an issue for government policy: to widen access. The disparities are huge: around 33 per cent of 18-year-olds, for example, go to university, but this percentage is in the 80s for higher social class groups and is less than 5 for children who have ever been in care. There is data to articulate this in detail. Policies need to be closely connected to schools. For example, if it is a target to widen access to Imperial College, then notice has to be taken of the fact that, on the one hand, a much higher percentage than average of potential students with three A-grade A-level science subjects come from independent schools; and on the other, that there are many schools in the state sector, particularly in inner city areas, that do not have an appropriate quota of specialist science teachers. The feasibility of government policy and possible new responses have to be tested in terms of detailed geographical analysis.

Education also now provides a good example of where joining up is essential: DCSF is responsible for schools, BIS for universities. Teacher-quality and system leadership are crucial to success. Can schools of education in universities and colleges deliver what is needed? And, of course, there is a third player – the Training and Development Agency (TDA): can they join up?

4.7.5 Health

Health is data-rich but data-disorganized. There have been a number of attempts, including the current and very expensive one, to systematize patient data and to create the underpinnings of what might finally be a patient-centred health care system. However, this is a good example of an area where we should not fall into the trap of waiting for 'perfect' data before good analysis can begin. Consider two ever-topical examples: the delivery of primary care; and the size and distribution of hospitals.

It is clear that GP practices vary enormously in size and efficiency. The ways in which hospital A&E services are used demonstrate failures in GP delivery. Some particular services – hearing and dentistry are obvious examples – are very poorly delivered by the NHS and have almost been given over to private practice to the detriment of those who cannot afford this. This territory is a good example of where the analysis needs to relate to two kinds of performance indicator: how a GP practice or a hospital is performing on the one hand; and the effectiveness of service delivery to people characterized by type and/or location. There will be instances where the performance of surgeries or hospitals is good but the delivery to sectors of the population is poor – illustrating our two kinds of performance indicator. The tools are available for this kind of analysis but the research is not being done. The controversy over polyclinics would dissolve if the case was presented on the basis of good analysis with a cost–benefit analysis that compared it to alternatives.

4.7.6 Housing

The bulk of housing policy is determined by the desire for home ownership and the market – and indirectly, therefore, by the planning system. For those who cannot afford to buy or raise a mortgage, the rental market takes over with a social market sector less populated by local authorities and more by housing associations. There is no good analytical overview that can tell the government the extent to which this system is working effectively – only cumulating anecdotal evidence. The tools are available to make this more systematic.

4.7.7 Food and environment

DEFRA has a wide-ranging agenda and issues list. Food prices rise and petrol prices rise, which will make it harder for people to access supermarkets where food is cheaper. (Already, out-of-town shopping centres are facing reductions in turnover.) So in this sense, they have some responsibility for access to a basic need. Geographers in the past have charted 'supermarket deserts'. But they also have responsibility for environmental quality – flood protection and coastal erosion at the sharp end of this – with connections to the major global issue of climate change. They have a good record, through the Environment Agency, for the analysis of flood risk. This could be extended to their wider territories.

4.7.8 Benefits, pensions, looking after the elderly

There are two hugely expensive and seemingly intractable problems that rest initially with DWP but also impact on other departments such as BIS, Health and, in relation to funding, the Treasury: benefit payments, particularly relating to unemployment and incapacity, and an increasingly ageing population, with challenges ranging from pensions to care provision. The costs to the government in these areas are staggering even though many responsibilities – the costs of care homes, for example – have been shifted to individuals and their families. There have been impressively massive studies: Lord Turner's on pensions and Lord Sutherland's on provision of care for the ageing, for example. But these have been considered mainly in the short term in relation to policy development – in both cases, the government was not able to accept the recommendations offered. These areas represent perfect examples of where simulations and projections through micro-simulation are easily feasible.

4.7.9 The criminal justice system

It is widely acknowledged that there are serious problems that run through all aspects of the criminal justice system, from knowledge of the incidence of crimes – most recently concerns about knife crime – through to apprehension, sentencing, prisons, probation and rehabilitation. Prison capacity is exceeded and it is very difficult for the government to respond quickly. How would a good information system help? There is considerable knowledge of the kinds of development support that would rehabilitate prisoners and reduce recidivism. Much good work is done in the Prison Service, the Probation Service and numerous charities. However, there is no electronic data system that enables the keeping track of prisoners, and, for example, matching them at sentence to a prison that would have appropriate facilities to support them. The proposed NOMIS system has been abandoned after much initial investment – further demonstrating what seems to have become almost impossible for the government: the effective delivery of large-scale IT systems.

There is an extensive catalogue of further problems. The provision of treatment for the mental health of prisoners is known to be poor. There is an inadequate supply of hostels for released prisoners. And since most crime is drugs-related, policies must take this into account. It would be an interesting cost–benefit analysis to explore a system that focused investment on support, treatment and rehabilitation rather than on expanding the numbers of prison places.

4.7.10 Transport

There is more systematic use of computer model-based analysis in this sector than any other. The challenge here is not in the deployment of tools, but in the policy and design elements of planning: what kinds of systems are appropriate for a future riddled with uncertainties on energy prices? The 'solutions' to the problem of providing good transport access on the one hand and reducing congestion on the other are usually seen to be a combination of the regulation of car travel through measures such as road pricing or the expansion of public transport. However, a proper analysis demands some integration with land-use planning. Exhortation to use public transport does not work! There are many situations where densities, especially in the suburbs, are too low to enable total travel times involving public transport to compete with the car, even on a congested road network. Analysis will reveal what is possible and what adjustments might be necessary in the future.

4.7.11 Energy

The government has an obvious responsibility for energy delivery and security. This is made more difficult by the fragmented nature of the industry following rounds of privatization followed by a series of takeovers. There is an obvious starting point: to model energy demand for both individual users and organizations and map this against different kinds of supply. This is a relatively straightforward modelling task but is almost certainly not being carried out in a systematic way – if at all.

4.7.12 Culture

Once the basics have been established – employment and income, housing, education, health and safety – the quality of life in a city is determined by its cultural opportunities. The relative levels of opportunities between cities is not a topic that has been systematically explored in research, nor has the analysis been carried out for groups within a city. This could be done with the techniques sketched here. There are also implications for the conservation and presentation of heritage sites in relation to the tourist industry, for example.

4.7.13 Joining up

Most of these issues are interconnected. Many of the problems are income-related. Poor income generates poor diet, poor health, poor performance in education, inadequate housing, the need for social welfare payments and, at the extreme, drugs-related crime. Poor diet exacerbates behaviour problems and connects to issues such as obesity. In general (leaving aside private means and, more importantly, pensions, for the time being) *adequate* income derives from employment. Government investment in large part relies on the tax take from employment. Well-paid employment demands skills. Skills are rooted in education. This picture is made more complicated by the changing mix of skills demanded in a rapidly developing knowledge economy. This places an emphasis on continuing education and lifelong learning. The Blair policy of 'education, education and education' may have been exactly right.

From a government perspective, decisions have to be made about what can be planned and what can be delivered through markets and private expenditure – supported by appropriate public investment in infrastructure and services and by regulation. Whatever this balance, even this level of decision-making needs to be informed by a CIS or a GovIS. Consider some specific examples – from many

– which illustrate the joining-up agenda.

We can begin at the local scale. *Planning systems* need to connect transport and land use and to integrate with economic strategies and local structures of public service provision. Some questions that are not easy to answer formally need to be tackled and decisions made: for example, will local investment in cultural facilities such as theatres and concert halls actually attract inward investment by companies? In planning and strategy terms, much progress has been made by many local councils. Interestingly, more thought is often applied to economic strategy than to town or city planning – the latter as a profession seeming to have fallen into inadequate control routines rather than the pursuit of imaginative design in an integrated way. Indeed, the recent Work Foundation report on cities found that the links between economic development and regeneration policies were, typically, not being made.

Social mobility has been a government concern in recent times. This is almost certainly rooted in the increasing social polarization of towns and cities. Real progress demands integrated policies embracing regeneration, education, health, criminal justice and rehabilitation and employment. There is a related problem of recruitment to public services: in many areas local housing is not affordable for the groups the government is trying to recruit.

At the national scale, the joining-up challenge begins with the fiscal and budget agendas. These in turn depend in part on future growth forecasts. These forecasts have to be placed in the context of globabilzation. There may be more changes to come, and there are risks to be assessed here. The Work Foundation report draws attention to the risk for cities that have had major expansions in financial services, that substantial chunks of these may be vulnerable to outsourcing to other countries. We have already posed issues that further imply questions, such as: if there is a predicted 2.5 per cent annual rate of growth, what does this upper-level constraint imply at local and regional levels? If public investments are the main levers of government policy, some major shifts appear to be needed which in turn must be integrated at a local level. Skills provision: does every town need a university? The answer is probably 'No!' – but the population of each place does need *access* to higher education. More prisons? Or better support to improve rehabilitation and reduce recidivism?

This argument has been, at best, illustrative. Many other examples could have been given. In all cases, however, it is likely that good analysis would support good decisions, and good analysis would support effective and convincing policy development and the inventiveness that leads to good solutions to problems. It is frustrating that such core analysis is not in place in central government and that central government is not supporting local government more effectively in this respect. It is unlikely even to be a resources issue. Much of the underpinning analysis could be developed on a central basis, paid for by building a budget from current efforts within departments and local authorities that are duplicating work on a large scale. Who could take on the role? The Office of National Statistics – except in that case, it may be a prisoner of old cultures – would find it difficult to take on the new? This could then be supported by research in a variety of environments and this would demand a substantial increase in the budget of the ESRC and, in varying degrees, the other research councils. This, in turn, would support university research on a 'big science' basis: a recognition that this kind of science is as important to the future development of the UK and its towns, cities and regions as the so-called 'hard' sciences, which are funded on a much more generous scale.

This territory represents research that is simultaneously basic and applied – indeed immediately applicable. This demands not only research council funding, but that universities have to be prepared to invest more in this kind of social science with new kinds of units that can support national government as well as their local communities. We need new kinds of university departments: 'The Kennedy School of Government' with science!

Ministers need to take the lead. If this is to be seen as a research problem in the short run – rather than as a governing issue, though it is that as well – then perhaps BIS as the department responsible for research could take the lead, with ministers supported by the Government Chief Scientific Adviser – who would also brief the Prime Minister – and by the Directors-General for Science and Research and for Higher Education. We might then begin to build effective underpinnings for evidence-based policy.

4.8 The arts and humanities

There are major unsolved problems and issues in the core disciplines: language evolution[41] and semiotics (which links to *structuralism* and the use of *metaphor*[42]) provide examples, and in each case the problems link to approaches in the social sciences.[43] It is interesting to explore issues of scale: to what extent would we expect to find novels about 'systems' as well as individual 'characters'? And there is considerable scope for conceptual shifts – again linking arts and social sciences – for example, in connecting history to what is often the same subject matter in the social sciences. What is the role of art in a post-skills era?[44] 'Art is the muscle of the imagination'[45] – and we need much of that muscle!

4.9 Integration: interdisciplinarity and big systems

The key question is: how can we link the traditional branches of knowledge to increase our knowledge power? It is already clear there is a need to explore what can be achieved through the linking of technologies that are currently largely the preserves of particular disciplines. A good example is the possibility of DNA-based computers. It becomes necessary to explore the linking of the silicon chip with biological molecules.[46] The essential part of the argument is the systems focus. The big systems, as we have seen in section 4.7 above, include cities, ecosystems, human bodies, local or national government, industries and medicine in relation to health services research and diagnosis.

A distinction is sometimes made between interdisciplinary and multidisciplinary working. The former represents fully integrated working (probably with superconcepts); the latter, people coming together from different disciplines and attempting to combine skills, the implication being in a less integrated way. The distinction is not a sharp one. There is a depth versus breadth issue at the root here: if we need the full depth, which can only be achieved by long training within disciplines, and if many disciplines have to be brought to bear in a subject like urban studies – the breadth – how can we hope to achieve full integration? Who are the paragons who can achieve interdisciplinary depth? The situation is further complicated by sociological and cultural dimensions: the hegemony of disciplines and the way this is reinforced institutionally in the UK, for example, by the Research Assessment Exercise.

For universities as the drivers of knowledge power, this agenda raises important questions. What are the most important and interesting topics to teach? How do we add knowledge power? How do we define the most effective research focus? What is going to make a difference? What is 'interesting' and 'important'?

These are subjective judgements – but they are judgements that have to be made. Not making them explicitly is a form of intellectual laziness.

These challenges also confront R&D and training in industry. A revolution in approach is needed. The ongoing task in Chapters 5, 6 and 7 is to confront these problems head on and to work out how things can be different – in the context of a variety of different kinds of organization!

Chapter 5

Requisite knowledge

We have discussed the developing knowledge base that will be found, or could be achieved, in academia. We now explore this from the perspective of organizations, focusing on the knowledge core, strategy for future development and the management structures and skills needed for delivery. This is all anchored in the concept of requisite knowledge.

5.1 Requisite knowledge

In an obvious sense, the world is made up of organizations. They can vary in size from the individual functioning as a one-person business or voluntary activity to the global conglomerate employing hundreds of thousands of people. So 'organization' is a generic term that embraces a huge range. Most of the immediate argument will be targeted on the knowledge needs of organizations in this broad sense. However, we also need to bear in mind the idea of different kinds of communities and, indeed, of individuals and we will explore these ideas in more depth in Chapter 8.

All organizations need knowledge power, and indeed, it is the business of some organizations to *deliver* knowledge power to others. Earlier, we introduced Ashby's law of requisite variety[1]: a control system needed to have at least as much variety as the system it was trying to control to be effective. This leads us to develop the concept of *requisite knowledge* for organizations: that amount of knowledge that organizations need to have to function effectively. What constitutes requisite knowledge? The whole argument of the book is directed towards the answer to this question! While there is a huge literature and store of knowledge, each of us can assemble a tool kit of core ideas and a set of complementary perspectives within a systematic framework that should provide an appropriate foundation. The core of this author's tool kit, as has been seen, stems from Ashby, and the notion of requisite knowledge, and then Harris, Andersson, Beer, Mintzberg and Christensen. The distilled ideas from the Cisco Education White Paper are important and can be generalized and, to help develop a template, an extension provided by Baghai, Coley and White (1999) also proves valuable. This leads to a framework with three main headings: the *knowledge core* (section 5.2), *strategy* (5.3) and *delivery* (5.4). In this chapter, we integrate the variety of ideas into this framework and this provides the basis for working through a range of examples in subsequent chapters.

It is useful to recall the key concepts of Chapter 3, to expand them where necessary, and then to elaborate on them in subsequent sections. The knowledge core is concerned with production technologies, demand through markets or clients and the business or organization's environment – knowledge of competitors and regulation.

Strategy relates to Harris's three components of policy (aims and objectives), design (invention) and analysis. There is a valuable elaboration of seven points that underpin strategic decisions by Baghai, Coley and White (henceforth BCW). These involve two other key ideas for the tool kit: that one element of strategy is about maintaining the present operation and the second is about developing it. The first two BCW notions are essentially concerned with 'maintenance': (1) existing products to existing customers and (2) finding new customers for existing products and services. The remaining five are concerned with 'development' (and hence, have a relation with Christensen's argument about new units). These are: (3) the development of new products and services, (4) new delivery approaches, (5) new geographies, (6) a new industry structure and (7) moving into new competitive arenas. This raises a whole set of questions about products and marketing, for example, and a good way to organize the answers is in a strategic plan.

The means of delivery is about management structure(s) and appropriately skilled staff. Andersson's 3 Cs idea (cognitive, creative and communications capabilities) and Beer's idea of an adequate information processing or intelligence system are important here. In devising management structures, Mintzberg's ideas come into play and it is important to relate any proposals to the appropriate parts of the Mintzberg diagram.[2]

What other parts of the management tool kit could be brought to bear? Oakland's business excellence model, introduced in Chapter 3, provides an overview. It is also interesting to translate the framework used in the Cisco Education White Paper, introduced in Chapter 1, into a broader context. Recall that it could be summarized as {R(T, C, A, L), S, P, Tech}: a reform package (R), that involved good teachers (T), the curriculum (C), accountability (A) and leadership (L). To this was added the skills (S) needed for the new century, appropriate pedagogy (P) and technology support (Tech). This would translate into a reform package consisting of (good staff, deciding the content of the business, accountability and leadership) coupled with twenty-first century skills, answers to the 'how?' questions and technology support.

When the analysis package and the strategy has been assembled, then appropriate funding has to be in place, for both maintenance and development (investment), together with the extent of outsourcing, partnerships and alliances, and human resources – and their management – all integrated in a *business plan*.

We now implement this preliminary analysis, first in section 5.2, discussing in turn the production technology (5.2.1), markets and clients (5.2.2), the environment (5.2.3), before proceeding to strategy (5.3) and delivery (5.4).

5.2 The core of requisite knowledge

5.2.1 The production technology

Once it is decided what constitutes the business or service of an organization, the idea of the production technology – how it can be delivered – is critical. This technology (and the associated decisions) determines the 'quality at a price' that will be on offer. The ability of the management to deliver effectively and efficiently is also critical and, indeed, the organizational structure could be considered to be part of the technology. Improvements, and some elements of competitive advantage, turn on investment in R&D and hence the knowledge base. In particular, there may be some monopolistic advantage if discoveries can be patented. This is particularly true, for example, of pharmaceutical companies. It is also at this stage of 'production function' thinking that other fundamental issues occur – in particular, the definition of core businesses and the extent to which parts of the production process should be outsourced. This has been a major trend in recent times – hence the rise and rise of business services – motivated from one or both of two directions. First, the supplier may be better at this part of the process because it is their core business, and they may have scale economies (so that the outsourced input is cheaper). Second, this may provide a better means of cost control. This emphasis on the supply chain and its articulation is the first component of what we have been calling the environment of the organization.

Technological change is very rapid and there is no doubt that innovation is crucial.[3] But Harvard Business School professor, Clayton Christensen, has identified what he calls the innovator's dilemma.[4] Christensen's argument is a very important one. In particular, new innovative technologies (which can include organizational change) are likely to be disruptive to the current staff. (This emphasizes the importance of culture in the workplace – an issue we will return to shortly.) So the dilemma is this: you need to adopt the new technologies to survive – but your staff will be so disrupted that it will not work, or you don't adopt and you don't survive anyway! The solution: deploy the new technologies in new units that can grow into new core businesses; the old core can be maintained, or even decline.[5] The new units become the means for expanding the capabilities of the organization. For convenience, we will call these 'Christensen units' and assign them superconcept status.

SC 101. Christensen units

Christensen, in his own summary (p. 226 et seq.), emphasizes other features of adopting new technologies: for example, the need to develop for new markets that often accompany them; the fact that it is often possible to proceed incrementally rather than through 'large and decisive investments'. We should emphasize in passing that 'technology' here should include the idea of 'soft technologies' – covering new ways of organizing businesses, for example. We return to these issues in the context of strategy and management later.

In earlier chapters, we have referred to the *knowledge explosion*. This is a fundamental problem for organizations, especially in relation to technology. How is it possible to keep up? There are implications here for:

- lifelong learning for staff (and finding ways of ensuring that the fruits of that are used within the organization);
- the use of such organizations as consultants, trainers and universities who may be better informed in particular fields;
- the need for some kind of 'war room' to assimilate and filter information and new knowledge – the Stafford Beer 'brain of the firm' argument.[6]

5.2.2 Markets and clients

Potentially, the organization now has 'products' and associated technologies. Who are these to be sold to? Who is to be served? In both consumer and public service cases, we will define the answer to these questions to be the *market* and translate the questions into: what is the market? And, of course, there is a circle in the argument here: there is a strong case for saying that the market should come first, or at least first equal.

The market will consist of either individual consumers (some possibly acting with, or on behalf of, households) or businesses. In some cases – computers, for example – both will apply. A usual first step is to estimate demand. Elementary economics tells us that this will be price-related. Quality is difficult to handle: are the two ends of the quality market in a product concerned with the same or different goods? Usually history provides a starting point in demand analysis, but in the case of a new product, there are severe difficulties for obvious reasons.[7] Once demand is estimated, a knowledge of competitors (or in the case of services, alternative providers) is needed to assess the impact of what is on offer – and this is the element of the environment drawn into the argument here. Third, a model of consumer behaviour is needed.

These three components are the key elements of a system model – the *flight simulator* in this instance. How many organizations even have the elements of such a model? Much of the analysis and content of Chapter 3 can be brought to bear here – from the building of computer system models to the deployment of the policy-design-analysis framework (to be developed further in 5.3 below). We will give many examples in subsequent chapters.

5.2.3 The environment

In 5.2.2, we noted the need for a comprehensive knowledge of markets, supply chains and competitors and what they achieve. All of this is needed to build the flight simulator. (A study of the competition is also a way of exploring alternative production functions: is anyone doing it better?) What is left, important for many industries, is knowledge of the *regulatory* environment. All this points to the need to integrate knowledge of how an organization can function most efficiently and effectively in its environment, and, where appropriate, how it can affect the environment – for example, in creating markets for new products.

5.3 Strategy

We saw earlier in our discussion of production technologies how important innovation is to ensure continuing growth[8] – or, at least, an appropriate response to changing technologies or a changing environment. Any organization needs a forward strategy. There is a voluminous literature on strategy. In our terms, we can focus on a set of superconcepts introduced in section 4.5 of Chapter 4: policy, design and analysis (PDA – SC 35). The policy component will include a clear statement of aims and objectives. The analysis component will include the application of the model – the flight simulator – to provide a 'What if?' forecasting capability. The design component is about inventing effective ways forward in the light of the policy and the analysis. The PDA framework is the foundation of strategy. The whole process is clearly iterative.

As we say in the introduction to this chapter, Baghai, Coley and White offer a valuable route to help make this process more explicit. In their case, they recognize that a company must balance 'the competing demands of running existing businesses and building new ones' – which we noted as the valuable distinction between *maintenance* and *development*.[9] They argue that an organization should operate on three *horizons*[10]:

1   extend and defend core businesses;
2   build emerging businesses; and
3   create viable options (which we can obviously take to mean the longer term).[11]

   SC 102. Planning horizons

They too emphasize the problems of overcoming inertia, but in looking for opportunities, they helpfully break the process down into seven steps (which in part correlates with Christensen's emphasis on new markets for new products). We repeat these for convenience here:

1   existing products to existing customers;
2   new customers;

3   new products and services;
4   new delivery approaches;
5   new geographies;
6   new industry structure;
7   new competitive arenas.

In discussing the development horizons, they again echo Christensen. This time they discuss capabilities and markets – but it is helpful to have their perspective: 'Executives who want to develop horizon 3 options into core profit engines face two big problems: market uncertainty and gaps in their skills, assets and relationships' (p. 71). They also argue later (p. 143) that one way forward is what they call 'disaggregation' – running the organization through 'small growth communities' and pushing 'leadership down into the organisation' – echoes of Christensen's 'new units'. Examples follow in the next two chapters.

5.4 Delivery: management structures and skills

There is a voluminous literature on management, as a visit to the appropriate section of any bookshop will show. Much of it is anecdotal, much of it is selling a particular recipe for success. Fortunately, some authors have distilled many of the key ideas and summarized them effectively. A particularly good example is Glass (1996). Another useful general model is that by Oakland (2000), which we introduced earlier with his business excellence model.[12] We should also recognize that there are many possible effective management styles for different kinds of organization.[13,14] Here, we take these basics as read and focus on the deeper problems that face most managers – uncertainty[15], the pace of change and the need for innovation (and all the traps that go with that).[16] We also take as read the fact that we all have to be lifelong learners in the acquisition of knowledge and the associated skills, and it is fashionable to concretize this goal at the organizational level and to argue that all organizations ought to be *learning* organizations. Again, there is a voluminous literature.[17]

Management in the broad sense should clearly embrace the strategy process described in the previous section. The starting point, therefore, is the assumption that the result of that process can be encapsulated in a strategic plan based on sound analysis. The management then needs to turn this into an operational or business plan: how to achieve the strategy. The approach adopted here is to focus on what have proved to be key authors in this writer's intellectual tool kit and then to use these to help elaborate the template for requisite organizational knowledge. We discuss in turn Andersson, Beer, Mintzberg and Christensen.

Recall Andersson's argument introduced in Chapter 1 about successful societies – C-societies – and in that context we noted that the same concepts could be applied to organizations. The key capabilities are cognitive, creative and communications.[18] This is another way of reminding ourselves of the need to ensure that the knowledge core is in place: the cognitive, together with an

R&D capability, the creative. It is the communications capability that is often neglected.

Second, recall the Beer argument from Chapter 3: the need for effective information processing capacity. This is particularly important in the context of the knowledge explosion and links to the building of communications capacities. Since no one organization will be able to keep up with everything, connections have to be made to networks of knowledge and there needs to be an in-house filter – the Stafford Beer model level 4 – to make the best of this.

Andersson and Beer provide a context. The third task is to ensure that an effective management structure is in place. We introduced the Mintzberg argument on structures (SC 85).[19] It is an important part of the knowledge base that structures can be characterized in an abstract, and therefore deeper and more general way, than is often presented. And if you accept some of the underlying sociology, then you learn something not only about organizational design, but also about constraints on such designs. If you are in a university or a hospital, for example, you learn that your management structure is less likely to work unless it effectively involves the front-line staff.

Fourth, recall the Christensen argument[20] from this chapter and the need for what we now call Christensen units to overcome disruptive new technologies. This is a convenient point with which to present this argument with a slightly different emphasis. Tushman and O'Reilly (1997) emphasize the 'benefits that accrue to a robust, stable and reliable organisation' (p. 11). But they also note (p. 29) that this is the recipe for success in stable environments and that failure as a result of inertia can result 'when environments shift'. They conclude that organizations have to be ambidextrous: 'managing for short-term efficiency by emphasising stability and control, as well as for long-term innovation by taking risks and learning by doing'.

SC 103. Ambidextrous organizations – short-run efficiency and long-run innovation

To make things work in an organization, to implement the strategy, a management structure and people with the appropriate skills are needed (policy, design and analysis skills again). It is worth noting that 'management' is for everybody in an organization – from the CEO to individual time-management for all staff – even if it is unplanned and by default.

Chapter 6

Knowledge power and universities

We have developed a general framework for requisite knowledge in organizations. We now consider what this means for the future development of universities. Universities – and colleges and other 'units' of higher education – are the engines of development of requisite knowledge for the economy and for society, but they also need their own requisite knowledge to be effective.

6.1 Introduction

The analysis so far has shown that the traditional 'containers' of knowledge are unlikely to meet the requisite needs of organizations. Neither the disciplines within a university nor the professional institutions that underpin many of the staffing structures of many organizations encourage the crossing of boundaries to put together integrated and requisite packages of knowledge. Universities have the potential to be the key providers and engines of knowledge power but to be effective, they will have to revolutionize themselves.

6.2 Towards radical change

Knowledge is a critical component for both economic and social development and universities are key engines of knowledge power. From an instrumental point of view, universities produce the skilled labour force – and through them, the knowledge power – needed by other organizations; they provide individuals with the basis of many of their life chances. Universities were, of course, often founded with instrumentalist objectives in mind, so there is nothing new in this. But as knowledge power becomes increasingly important, universities have to find ways of simultaneously maintaining traditions of critical independence with directly utilitarian, indeed commercial, objectives – reconciling their economic and social goals.

Universities traditionally transfer knowledge into the economy through their graduates and postgraduates and through the outcomes of research – and the twenty-first century skills agenda is very important in this respect. Increasingly, outreach activities are more directly organized: *lifelong learning* provision for corporate organizations (rather than as, traditionally, for individuals) and in both *applied research* (essentially outsourced from organizations) and *technology transfer* through licensing or the development of university companies – all new forms of knowledge transfer.[1] There are also opportunities for *translational research* and *consultancy*. Knowledge power will also be enhanced through the development of electronic networks such as virtual science parks – the collaborative power of Web 2.0. This will help create enhanced cognitive, creative and communications capacities and universities will be key nodes in such networks – important elements in the digital nervous system.[2]

The education system will have to generate the people required to provide requisite knowledge power. This begins to define the challenge for universities. There may be an issue of the speed at which the school system can respond in order to deliver the necessary input, especially since this means solving the deprived area/inner city problem, and we return to this issue below.[3] There are also deeper issues within the organization of universities themselves – with too much emphasis on traditional discipline boundaries and too little interdisciplinary work.

It is useful as a starting point in this case to return to the Cisco code – {R(T, C, A, L), S, P, Tech} – and apply these concepts to universities, and then to connect these ideas through the templates of Chapter 5. We will use the UK as our main example, but conclusions, *ceteris paribus*, can be drawn for other university systems. It should be noted at the outset that universities are different from schools in two fundamental ways. First, education post-18 is not compulsory and so universities have to attract their students; and second, universities carry out research as well as teaching – and indeed, as in the case of medicine and teaching hospitals, professional services as well.

We begin by reviewing, broadly, university teaching. In the UK, the university equivalent of the education 2.0 reforms – the R(T, C, A, L) have been largely accomplished, mainly through strong devolution of responsibilities, placing universities in a competitive framework with appropriate accountability for government funding. A generation of leaders has emerged to drive this system, and much more attention is paid to the nurturing of university staff in their teaching roles. Curriculum innovation is at best patchy, however. Less progress has been made towards an education 3.0 model. There has been some progress with the skills agenda – rooted in the Enterprise programmes of the early 1990s. There has been some progress with pedagogy in the sense of transition from blackboards to PowerPoint, and through the JISC programme[4], but the essentials – the university lecture, for example – remain the same. It may be, then, that not enough has been made of the potential for support from new (e.g. Web 2.0) technologies. There has probably been far less use of equipment such as interactive whiteboards in universities relative to schools, for example. However, the internet has made a substantial impact – as an addition to, even in some cases almost a replacement for, libraries in some areas.

It is also interesting, and more challenging, to apply the {R(T, C, A, L), S,

P, Tech} framework to the other half of the traditional university role – that is, research. Accountability (A) and leadership (L) do not present a problem – encapsulated in the Research Assessment Exercise in the UK, now to be followed by the Research Excellence Framework.[5] The 'teachers' (T) become 'researchers' – often the same people – and the quality questions are of the same order. The 'curriculum' becomes the 'research agenda' and here there are major issues of choice – particularly in relation to the economy and its needs. What should the balance be between 'blue skies' research and something more applied? The skills agenda (S) in this case links closely with the curriculum (C). What should the priorities be in research and what kinds of skills are needed? The 'Tech' dimension is interesting: internet tools provide the basis for effective collaborative research on a global scale.

Third, we can apply the Cisco code to universities' third-stream activities and this helps reveal the scale of the task. However, a preliminary comment is in order: all third-stream activities – give or take professional services – are essentially teaching or research, but to new constituencies or for new users. By characterizing these as 'outreach' or as 'third stream', they become marginalized. It will be better to think of universities in the future as expanding their reach in relation to their core activities. Nonetheless, we can use the Cisco code to explore what is involved in these extensions. The C and S components – curriculum and twenty-first century skills – involves universities defining the mutual knowledge agenda for themselves with employers and employees. The T represents the community that will teach it – and this is a non-trivial question because, without a major cultural change, it will not be the bulk of the present academic staff (who will not see this as a prime component of their role). The Christensen argument then kicks in here: set up new units and recruit new staff for this role, drawing in the more traditional resources of the university as appropriate. The P and the Tech – the pedagogy and the supporting technology – raise interesting questions too. It is reasonably straightforward for a university to run MBA courses in business schools. But it is also necessary to recognize that the bulk of the 'students' will be located far from campus, and so the technology of distance delivery – ideally within a blended learning system – becomes relevant. Accountability is quite hard and undeveloped – though this would not be difficult at the level of counting students. What is needed is strong and imaginative leadership both in universities and among employers to make all this happen.

We can now relate this analysis to the template of Chapter 5 and apply this to universities as organizations. C, and to an extent, S are the *knowledge core*. T, P and Tech represent the *production* technology. A represents the *environment*. These three topics are developed in sections 6.3–6.4.

As we have noted, the Cisco framework neglects, in the university context, the market: for students and for research. And this connects closely to the idea of extended 'reach'. In the case of schools, the 'market' is relatively well defined because of compulsory education. What should be the breadth of the student constituency? How should universities contribute to lifelong learning and employer engagement? What is the market for research? These market questions are pursued in section 6.5 below. These are questions of strategy development and are explored in section 6.6. How the strategy is delivered and what this implies both for management structures and government support is discussed in section 6.7.

6.3 The knowledge core

Universities have two elements to their knowledge core: the form of their product, which is essentially knowledge – and this raises all the questions about packaging, interdisciplinarity and so on – and knowledge about themselves, including their production technology. We consider these steps in turn.

In Chapter 2, we laid out a model of the knowledge space; in Chapter 4, we began to articulate the changing knowledge agenda for teaching and research in universities – in the present context, the 'product'. As we have seen, universities have three main activities: teaching, research and knowledge transfer. The last is something of a catch-all, embracing traditional activities such as clinical medicine and being a provider of lifelong learning and continuing professional development (CPD), applied research – in the context of increasing company outsourcing of research and training – and direct knowledge transfer of the products of university research. (And, of course, there is a more traditional kind of knowledge transfer in the production of graduates and postgraduates.) These all involve different elements of the knowledge core – essentially Andersson's three Cs: cognitive, creative and communications.

Should universities simply respond to demand? Or, indeed, as many would argue, to their traditions? Or is there some broader national interest here? It is an implicit argument of Chapter 4 that universities need to ask fundamental questions about the structure of knowledge, how it should be taught and how it should be developed – the content of teaching and research programmes. There are very good reasons for change and development. First, that relative to the traditional academic disciplines, the structures of knowledge are now essentially interdisciplinary. In practice, this may well mean that new disciplines have to evolve – perhaps led by the professions such as business or medicine. Second, there is the knowledge explosion. Not everything can be 'learned' and so it is necessary to shift to a higher level of learning while still achieving depth – the capability to cope with difficulty – as well as breadth.[6] Can skills and frameworks be taught in such a way that an individual's knowledge can then be effectively complemented by expert systems or knowledge management systems? Internet information sources are a highly imperfect first step in this direction – offering breadth but not depth.

We pursue the issues of how to bring about radical change in the 'production technology' of teaching below.

The research agenda demands an answer to the question: how does one effectively formulate research problems? This is a combinatorial challenge. The outcome is complex. Ziman writes of 'a bewildering variety of institutions' or the 'organisational kaleidoscope'.[7] The challenge for funders of research in universities

– and for universities themselves, of course – is how to answer the questions: what is interesting and what is important? Foresight exercises help, but are usually conservative. Chapter 4 has offered the beginnings of a map.

6.4 The production technology

The production technologies in teaching are understood – at least in traditional terms of lectures, tutorials, libraries and labs. Costs have been driven down in the UK in recent times and it is not known where the limit comes when traditional methods cease to work well – and indeed whether there is anything to replace them effectively. What is not yet well understood is the efficacy of electronic delivery, though there are many experiments in progress.[8] We should assume, however, that technology will transform the production function. Lectures, for example, will become available electronically on a global basis. Why listen to someone local and possibly ineffective when a global star is available on the internet? Why should the university supply the local lecturer? It can use those resources for other means of student support. Technology can deliver new models!

There is some experience of the teaching of research methods, but I suspect that little is known about how effective they are and whether there are alternatives. It is perhaps significant that many of the major discoveries in a number of fields are made by those who have migrated from other areas. Multidisciplinarity may well be crucial – and indeed this is a primary argument, as should already be clear, of this book.

6.5 The environment

Universities now work in an environment that is part competitive, part regulated[9] and indeed part protected, because only universities can award degrees and this gives them some quasi-monopolist powers. (There are now beginning to be exceptions: in England, companies are eligible for degree-awarding powers.)[10] However, because of the previous government interest in maintaining quality in universities at lower prices[11], strong quality assessment regimes are in place. The Research Assessment Exercise (RAE) seriously biases university behaviour. The market for students has been, until recently, a seller's market: there were more potential students than places each year. The system has now been expanded to a level where this is no longer self-evidently the case. This further complicates the marketing issue. And there has been a fall in demand for mathematics-based courses, especially the so-called STEM subjects – science, technology, engineering and mathematics, for example.[12] There are challenges, therefore, on many fronts.

6.6 Demand: markets and clients

Much is known about traditional demand – 18-year-olds from middle-class households – but much less about other groups. New markets are continually being developed and tested through widening participation programmes and different kinds of lifelong learning. There has been no systematic study of markets – something an intelligent retailer might undertake as a matter of course! This would now be possible using the modelling methods discussed in earlier chapters.[13] One advantage of such an analysis is that attention would be focused on appropriate performance indicators: on university performance and on delivery of higher education to people by area of residence.

There is one particular issue to which we should draw attention. The flow of students into universities depends critically on the performance of the schools' system. That quality in turn depends on the teachers. Most teachers are trained, and receive their continuing education, through universities. So the argument turns full circle and there is a clear implication that universities should pay special attention to this, both in their own interest as well as in the national interest. Schools' performance is very polarized – much excellent, much awful – and so there is a serious challenge here for universities.

6.7 Strategy

It is fruitful, as usual, to begin with the policy-design-analysis (PDA) framework. We have, at least implicitly, argued that universities need to respond to a new knowledge agenda and so this must be a key objective. The underpinning analysis is represented in Chapters 1–4. Second, they need a good understanding of their client base in the developing knowledge economy. Good analysis should underpin an objective to serve this diverse base. The design task is then to ensure that the structures, facilities and staffing are in place to deliver the objectives in the light of the analysis. This is where some radical thinking is needed and we pursue this through the BCW framework – a review of the seven steps follow:

1   Universities have been more than adequate at 'selling' existing courses to (in a broad sense) existing customers.
2   They have been pretty good at finding new customers for these products or variants of them.
3   They have been less good at developing new products and services in the teaching area while at the same time,
4   being spectacularly good at generating new research – albeit it in overly-narrow, discipline-based areas.[14]
5   They have been pretty good at 'new geographies', with big increases in the UK of numbers of international students.
6   We have already seen that much research needs to be done on new delivery methods, ultimately leading to a new 'business' model.
7   They have responded well in competing with each other, but major questions remain about whether universities will cope well against global competition. For example, will 'for profit' professional trainers take the bulk of the CPD market? Will major pharmaceutical, biotech, electronics and IT companies

become the main sources of research in these areas because the companies can afford better labs and can 'buy' the best people? The answers to these questions are not necessarily 'Yes', but they do define areas where serious strategic thinking is needed.

The critical questions lie at (3), (4) and (6). Can universities be bold enough to redraw the map of knowledge to offer knowledge power in new courses – new 'products' – and can they move fast enough to remain at the research front line in the future? The trend towards larger units – faculties rather than discipline-based departments – should facilitate the right kinds of thinking. It is also necessary to develop cross-faculty interdisciplinary institutes.[15] Can they develop effective new delivery models? The forces of conservatism in these matters tend to keep the bulk of the funding to support traditional departments and so we devote a section to funding issues below. Fundamental management and cultural change will be needed and we now turn to these issues.

6.8 Delivery: management structures and staffing

Universities, at best, remain arenas of critical thinking and of collegiality with increasingly professional management. This has facilitated a shift to decentralized structures – conforming with management fashion but often in an innovative way.[16]

In Mintzberg terms, universities (like hospitals) are certainly professional bureaucracies – though for some of their newer activities, they need to be more fleet of foot, say, like management consultants and therefore more like, in part, what Mintzberg calls adhocracies. A corollary of this argument is that the 'front line workers', such as university professors, will want, in principle, a say in the management and hence the commitment, in many institutions, to collegiality.

The Mintzberg diagram helps us in a number of ways. There are certainly areas – medicine being the most obvious example – where stringent standards have to be maintained for the public good and this implies having an effective technostructure – in the UK's case, through external involvement of the General Medical Council.

A programme of radical development is called for on the basis of this analysis. At the same time, it is important – through a version of the Christensen 'disruptive technologies' argument – not to lose the basis of what universities currently have, most of which is valuable. The four keys are:

1   structures
2   funding
3   staffing
4   management.

Universities, as we have noted, have traditionally had two main activities: teaching and research. They are very different but it has been customary to carry them out with the same staff. This has some obvious advantages, often summarized in the phrase 'teaching in an atmosphere of research'. In some parts of universities, there has always been a third arm: the clinical work of medics, continuing education work, applied research, and the setting up of university companies or the licensing of intellectual property. All this represents different forms of *outreach* and can all be summarized, as we have seen, under the more technical term *knowledge transfer*. In principle, therefore, there are three kinds of activity being carried out by the same staff.

The core of a university organizational *structure* is the set of faculties, schools and departments, mainly based on academic disciplines. There are interdisciplinary centres and institutes, but these are typically much smaller. We have seen that there is a sea change in the map of important research problems and in the set of skills needed to tackle these – and, indeed, through restructured teaching programmes, in the set of skills needed for graduates to function effectively in many kinds of employment. In the last case – work – employers can provide their own training (though with the danger that this is too narrow for longer run objectives). In the university case, this is not being done in an analogous way because the perception that the research map has changed is not there. There is, however, such a perception outside universities by the customers of much university research. Research councils, for example, are now largely organized on interdisciplinary lines, although industry is clearly not organized in a way that maps on to academic disciplines. Hence, organizing and structuring to respond to the challenges of interdisciplinarity is a key issue.

What we might expect to find in the future, therefore, is more division of labour between teaching, research and knowledge transfer, and more emphasis on interdisciplinary work. However, the strength of disciplinary cultures, discussed in Chapter 3, makes it very difficult to do this on the scale and at the speed that is required. There is also a sense in which the Christensen response can already be seen in the creation of large numbers of interdisciplinary centres and institutes.[17] However, this is where universities face another difficulty: rapid change costs money and so *funding* for investment in restructuring is critical. The centres and institutes are largely underfunded compared to traditional schools and departments, and universities are operating within such tight margins that it is difficult to find the money for this kind of academic investment. And this implies a threat, already hinted at earlier, that other institutions, such as independent or industrial research labs, will be the agents of innovative development and universities will be left behind.

It is the third-arm agenda that demands an almost wholly Christensen response: that is, the need for new institutions and units within the university. This raises issues of structure, funding and staffing. We have already discussed the possibly inadequate division of labour between teaching and research. Consider the third-arm agenda in this respect: a different kind of research – applied research on relatively short time-scales, and some consultancy; a different kind of teaching, possibly with different delivery methods to different kinds of students; and building university companies to support any of these purposes. Some academics will take to this agenda – the academic entrepreneurs – but typically they have to be located in units outside their schools and departments. In general, it will be necessary to recruit different kinds of staff to work in new kinds of units. These might be applied-research units, largely industrially funded; institutes for corporate learning, supporting lifelong learning agendas in large organizations – possibly through corporate universities; or university companies built either on research-based patented discoveries or on clusters of expertise.

Again, there is a funding problem. The possibilities are support through large contracts with properly funded overheads[18] and/or some capital investment. There are examples of each, sometimes with quite innovative structures, but the scale of activity is too small compared to what is needed. We need to explore the funding issues further before we address management.

The main sources of funding (oversimplifying, of course) are:

1   fees and government funding per student;
    a   home/EU and overseas;
    b   third arm – full fee, CPD etc;
2   research grants and contracts;
    a   basic;
    b   applied;
3   core research support for overheads and infrastructure;
4   income from specialized knowledge transfer activities – particularly licensing and university companies;
5   capital grants for teaching and research infrastructure;
6   loans, mainly for buildings;
7   other – e.g. equity, joint ventures – potentially a major step forward for third-arm developments.

Donations may be significant in some cases but are neglected here in this business-focused analysis. What is largely absent is equity funding – the exception being some investments in university companies.

Structures (in large universities at least) will be decentralized and delivery will be through the units discussed earlier – the universities' SBUs[19]:

• faculties, schools and departments, largely discipline-based – DBUs;
• interdisciplinary centres and institutes – IDUs;
• third-arm units – TAUs.

Figure 6.1 shows the income streams generated by and supporting the different units.

This table is revealing. Discipline-based units are substantially funded from (home/EU) student numbers, research grants and contracts and research support.

	1		2		3	4	5	6	7
	a	b	a	b					
DBUs	X	x	X	x	X		y	y	
IDUs	x		X	x	x			y	
TAUs		X	x	X		X			x

Figure 6.1 Income streams in higher education.

Key: X = main funding source; x = minor funding source; y = occasional funding source; for column headings see bulleted list on previous page.

Interdisciplinary units are typically funded from research grants and contracts, with minor funding from (usually postgraduate) student numbers. A major planned innovation is to seek out interdisciplinary fields where the research frontier links to potential undergraduate recruitment. This would improve the financial base, as in DBUs. Third-arm units derive their income from some mixture of – and usually not all of – full-fee (usually CPD) students, applied research and from technology transfer activities.

We can finally address the *management* implications of this analysis. The argument of the previous sections indicates desirable directions of development and there are some clear implications. First, IDUs would be stronger with an undergraduate base. Second, the available capital in columns 5 and 6 should be used to restructure and develop DBUs where necessary and accelerate the development of IDUs. The TAUs need more 'equity' funding, which can probably be achieved mainly through joint ventures with universities offering intellectual capital and partners offering complementary skills and financial capital.

All units need plans and futures in which they are properly financed with strong independent managements, functioning within the boundaries of corporate priorities. Central units are needed to help plan the necessary restructuring and development – an Academic Development Unit – and to help secure partnerships and funding for the more rapid development of third-arm units.

An interesting end point to this part of the discussion is to check against the Andersson and Beer superconcepts. Universities are probably supreme in terms of cognitive capacities, at least in relation to traditional disciplines, and they have considerable creative capabilities, but not typically about themselves! Their communications capacities in terms of outreach are traditionally not good, and this is a key to the development of the third-arm agenda. Like most organizations, they would be better informed with an appropriate Beer level 4 information system.

6.9 A radical shift

All of this adds up to an agenda for rapid development and change in universities. But will it happen? The Christensen challenge is paramount here: the core staff are in traditional departments and, particularly in terms of teaching, will often feel threatened by a shift to interdisciplinarity. This also encourages students to be conservative. There was an attempt in Leeds to launch Informatics courses that married computer science with different kinds of modelling – but there were few takers. There was the feeling that students felt safer with a traditionally labelled course. So while there is clearly a need for more risk taking in course offerings, it will not be easy. It ought to be much easier in relation to applied research, especially for public services, to meet the agenda outlined in Chapter 4. What is likely to happen is that a small number of enterprising universities will find a way of leading and, eventually, others will follow.

What would these enterprising universities be doing? A radical shift in structure and commitment is needed. The traditional university business can continue – with new curricula to respond to the knowledge explosion. It should be possible to add, some or all in a particular university – a College of Lifelong Learning, a College of Corporate Learning and a company, let's say University Consultants PLC – to take on the larger aspects of the new agenda. This would ensure new kinds of staff who were committed to responding creatively to the needs of individual lifelong learners, to the needs of organizations and to the delivery of knowledge services. At least the last two of the three could, in principle, be profit-making and could be equity-financed.

Chapter 7

Employers in the knowledge economy

7.1 Introduction

Employers, particularly large ones, in some senses have to be their own 'university'[1]: they have to work out the means by which they and their employees can acquire and maintain the requisite knowledge needed for their company. This is usually seen as 'training' rather than 'education', though there are exceptions to this. Much of the training is typically organized through the HR department and is seen as an HR responsibility. A valuable starting point for a new appraisal of training and employee education needs will be the Cisco code followed by the BCW template.

We can start with the Cisco code that we generalized in Chapter 5.

{R (T, C, A, L), S, P, Tech}

becomes

{staff, the business what?, accountability, leadership, skills, how?, technology support}.

As usual, the 'what?' and 'skills' involve the specification of requisite knowledge. We should make the obvious point here that the skills dimension of this should include the element of 'learning capacity', which then offers a kind of future proofing. Accountability might relate to outputs – results – rather than simply inputs. The 'staff', 'how?' and 'technology' is all about delivery: the extent to which this is in-house or achieved through external trainers – possibly through relationships with universities. Strong leadership will be needed for this to be lifted beyond the routine and too often mundane.

We proceed in subsequent sections by example – retail, manufacturing, consultancy, and government and public services – on the basis of the key BCW elements.

7.2 Retail and consumer services

7.2.1 Introduction

'Retail' in a narrow sense refers to shopping; in a broader sense, it embraces all services to customers. Hence, the concept of 'retail banking': banks have exactly the same issues as retailers in locating branches, for example. But the concept can also be extended to, for example, airlines. Their 'locations' may be largely fixed – at airports – but they still have to decide what services (routes) they are offering and from where to where. Thus, there are generic ideas that apply very widely, although they will obviously have to be refined in particular contexts.

7.2.2 The knowledge base

The production 'technology' is made up of:

- products for sale (and a knowledge of the associated supply chain);
- the infrastructure – typically a branch network;
- the staff;
- and a knowledge of the market and the means of marketing.

This framework is well defined. The difficult task is to assemble the components in an effective way. Some organizations succeed; many do not. This is a good example of where a 'What if?' forecasting capability – the 'flight simulator' – can be assembled. It is possible to build computer models of demand by small area and of the supply – as a representation of the 'attractiveness' of outlets and to predict the assignment of the demand to the supply.[2] This is initially done for the current system – say, as a computer model of a retail sector for a city region or indeed for the whole country. Such a model can be deployed in two ways. First, it can be used as a planning tool; second, it can be used on behalf of one retailer who might wish to optimize a branch network. In this latter case, of course, it has to be assumed that other retailers do not respond![3] In this case, the flight simulator is the core of much of the potential role of Beer's level 4, though it is important for it to be a part of senior management's tool kit and not simply that of the market analysts!

7.2.3 Strategy

We can begin as usual with the BCW framework:

1   Existing products to existing customers. This is likely to be the core of any retail business, recognized in the management literature under such headings as customer relationship management (CRM).
2   New customers. In a given situation, this is one of the objectives of the marketing department as a means of growing the business. It is also a key part

of the strategy to optimize the branch network, and in particular to consider opening new branches to attract new customers, and the simulation model can be used as an aid in this process.

In each of these cases, the effectiveness of the product portfolio relative to those of competitors needs to be tested. The production technology will be continually changing. The assessment of this portfolio will need skills in business, as in market assessment, design and technology. The analysis will also provide the basis for the following:

3 The possibility of new products and services.
4 The industry's own technology is the basis of new delivery approaches, and this will embrace, for example e-retailing through the internet, a wholly different technology to that involved in branch retailing.
5 'New geographies' in this context is essentially a marketing question.
6 A new industry structure? An example of a fundamental change is what has become known as *disintermediation*, that is, cutting out the 'middle men' whether wholesalers or brokers (as in insurance, for example).
7 New competitive arenas – competitors with new products or new delivery technologies?

All these headings imply a whole set of questions about products, delivery channels and marketing. The analysis will throw up some major strategic questions. Should the branch network consist of a small number of large branches or a large number of small ones? Should there be a hierarchy of branches? How would the network structure relate to the hierarchical structure of service centres in cities and regions? Should there be more than one branch in a large city centre?

These questions relate to some of the superconcepts discussed in Chapter 4: hierarchy, network, interaction and location. The answers to these questions will depend on a knowledge of consumer behaviour in a particular sector and of the character of the geographical region being studied.

7.2.4 Delivery: management structures and staffing

In Mintzberg terms, the structure is likely to be divisional, with divisions based partly on function (product?) and partly on geography. In retail, of course, there are many small single branch businesses with correspondingly simple structures. The more interesting cases are the large organizations with possibly hundreds or even thousands of outlets. The Mintzberg structure[4] illuminates the issue and is repeated here in adapted form for convenience as Figure 7.1.

The strategic questions are those of the previous subsection and some of the decisions will be recorded in the technostructure – particularly about the quality of products, for example.[5] There will also have to be a strategy for the network of outlets, a structure of middle management (including support services such

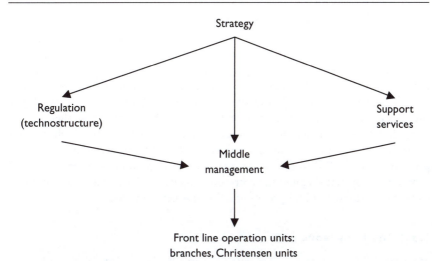

Figure 7.1 Organization structure.

Source: Adapted from Figure 1.2 in Mintzberg, M. (1983) *Structure in fives*, Prentice-Hall, Englewood Cliffs, NJ.

as training) and the staffing of the outlets (which constitute the front line in this case).

In some cases, alliances will be very important – as with airlines, for example. The equivalent of a 'branch' for an airline is a combination of airports and routes. Alliances can potentially add passengers to particular routes by expanding ongoing connectivity at destinations.

Staff in the retail business need an interesting mixture of skills. They have to know enough about *technology* to understand their products, particularly from a quality perspective; they have to have distinctive flair and hence *design* skills; and of course, they have to have *business* skills. (Recall the different kinds of thinking involved in these different types of skills – cf. Chapter 3.) Their business skills will be supported by the 'simulator'. They will have to be aware of new delivery technologies. They are living in a rapidly changing field with new competitors emerging continually. The history of companies such as Marks & Spencer shows that nothing can be taken for granted. There are implications here for the demand for a new kind of university course that offers and integrates these skills.

7.3 Manufacturing

7.3.1 Introduction

Universities, retail systems and public services all operate within a global knowledge economy (and some retailers have global operations – like Wal-Mart) but in the main they have national and more local manifestations. Much manufacturing is truly global, especially in fields of commodity production – like printed circuit boards. What is interesting in terms of the argument of this book, what is at the heart of, for example, hi-tech companies, is *systems* knowledge. The outsourcing of manufacturing to low-wage economies like China is commonplace, but you can now find examples even of the outsourcing of design. What remains at the HQ of the operation is the knowledge of how to put the whole system together.

Against this background, we should begin with the question: what is the importance of manufacturing in a modern *national* economy? If an increasing proportion of GDP is in the service or post-service sectors, is an economy still driven by manufacturing and the corresponding export base? This issue could be tackled by analysis and interpretation of input–output models.

7.3.2 The knowledge base

Manufacturing, more than other sectors, is literally dependent on its production technology. In formal terms, we need to account for the input resources needed to implement it: raw materials, land, labour and capital. The 'raw materials' in this case can include sophisticated products that make up elements of the supply chain. Then, of course, manufacturers need to understand their market. Often, this will be a business-to-business market, very different from consumer markets discussed earlier. It is still possible, however, to produce effective information systems.

What is increasingly important, as we noted in the introduction, is the systems knowledge that underpins the manufacturing process. In engineering, for example, sectors like aerospace and defence, automobiles, construction and building materials all need *systems* approaches.

There are two key elements of the knowledge core, both technologically based: first, that which enables low-cost manufacturing – price being the competitive advantage; second, the knowledge that gives competitive advantage on the basis of patentable technology, ideally something which is unique. The Cisco code provides a means of summarizing what has to be done. Recall that in its generalized form it is:

> {staff, the business what?, accountability, leadership, skills, how?, technology support}.

The key points in this case must be to have a mix of staff with appropriate skills who can both run the business ('maintenance') and be connected to the R&D technology frontier ('development') to ensure that the business keeps up with the game, and even gets ahead of the game.

7.3.3 Strategy

The BCW questions in some respects are simpler for manufacturing. The 'maintenance' questions – 'existing products to existing customers' and 'new customers'

– involve basic B2B marketing. What is usually critical in this case, given the pace of technological change, is the R&D base, which will generate new products and services. 'New industry structure' can also be important as particular sectors globalize and commodify. (Globalization and the search for effective low-cost manufacturing capacity is part of the 'new geographies' agenda for manufacturing.) Failure to respond in product development and to any industry restructuring will lead to serious competitive problems. Large companies, through scale economies, can more easily afford R&D than small ones. And yet in many sectors, it is argued that it is the relatively small companies that are the most innovative, and that the large companies then, in various ways, cherry pick the best ideas – through licensing or company purchase.[6]

The emphasis in the argument so far has been, not surprisingly, on technology. In manufacturing, however, there is also considerable weight to be given to financial structures and this has implications both for the knowledge base and for the management skills that are needed. The core of this part of the argument is two-fold: that much investment will be funded through the stock market; and that the company's share price will be both a key performance indicator for management and a reflection of the market's confidence in the company. The share price is determined by a combination of past performance and the market's judgement about prospects for the future – a different kind of 'What if?' forecasting.

7.3.4 Delivery: management structures and staffing

Manufacturing companies exhibit many different structures – probably virtually all of the 'Mintzberg types' – from the family firm with a simple or 'machine' structure to the divisionalized on either sector or geographical bases. However, the core of management skill in manufacturing beyond the technological knowledge base is largely generic and is well represented in the management literature.

7.4 Integrating knowledge: the consultancy business

7.4.1 Introduction

A theme of this book is that it is necessary to integrate the elements of knowledge for any particular purpose. We have also seen that it is very difficult to do this within any one organization. We can perhaps begin, therefore, to explain the success of the consultancy business: consultants are knowledge integrators, knowledge miners. Ideally, they should be able to articulate the concept of requisite knowledge for their clients. In practice, much of their core business is the provision of low-cost efficient services for companies who want to outsource.

We should begin our analysis by setting the scene through anticipating one of the BCW strategic questions about industry restructuring because this shows some interesting trends in the direction of integration. There are a number of

dimensions to this. Traditionally, professional business service firms have oper-
ated within their defined professional fields – such as law and accountancy – but
the necessity for integration has led increasingly to professions coming together:
large firms are offering a comprehensive service. Second, as we have seen in earlier analyses, there is an increasing tendency to outsource. This makes obvious
sense in relation to areas like payroll or IT if it can be demonstrated that this
is a 'commodity' purchase – that it is cheaper to buy 'electricity' than to run
one's own power station. But it also makes sense in relation to the purchase of
specialist knowledge. Whether, for many organizations, outsourcing has gone
too far in this respect is a matter for continuing debate. The scale of fees paid to
consultants by major corporations – public and private – begs the question as to
whether these resources would have been better deployed building up internal
knowledge power.

7.4.2 The knowledge base

A major consultancy should have access to the basic skills in management, organization development, finance, IT, the environment and education (in relation to
staff development and training), and perhaps law. The core disciplines that are
fundamental are economics and geography (from local to global scales) together
with the whole bundle of disciplines associated with technology. (The technology
knowledge is likely to be compartmentalized into specialist *sector* knowledge.)
However, what should be emphasized is systems thinking and systems knowledge
and this in turn implies an interdisciplinary perspective. Many of the superconcepts
introduced in earlier chapters then come into play: systems modelling, mathematical modelling and simulation[7], informatics and improved performance indicators
rooted in cost–benefit analysis. It is difficult for any one organization to encompass
such a broad area and this emphasizes the need for communication skills within
the 3Cs bundle.

7.4.3 Strategy

The BCW analysis applies to consultants as much as anyone else. The sale of existing products to existing customers, particularly in outsourcing, gives longer term
stability in an environment where many contracts are by their nature short-term.
New customers are obviously important as are new products and services – the
latter very much the result of being at the heart of the knowledge revolution. The
consultancy business operates at global and local scales and so already encompasses
all geographies.

7.4.4 Delivery: management structures and staffing

In Mintzberg[8] terms, consultancies are usually adhocracies because they are
made up at any one time of constantly changing project teams, and this demands

particular kinds of management skill. However, the real challenge of management for a consultancy is to deliver requisite knowledge and organizational structures to clients. So the checklist comes into play for clients as much as for themselves. For example: review delivery of appropriate cognitive, creative and communications capacities; the extent of devolution; the extent of outsourcing; partnerships and alliances; the means of handling complexity; and this includes joined-upness and other kinds of connectivity, as well as performance management. The Andersson-Beer-Mintzburg-Christensen dimensions would have to be worked out in each case.

7.5 Government and public services

7.5.1 Introduction

Government is concerned with, in the terms in Chapter 2, the big systems: demography, economics, infrastructure, environment and the major public services. The underpinning knowledge base should be the best of what the social sciences have to offer. We charted out this agenda in some detail in Chapter 4. However, the social sciences in many ways have not concerned themselves effectively enough with the problems, and government at all levels has typically shown neither the understanding nor the patience to seek out these underpinnings. There is a tremendous resource deployed in government, but it is somehow disparate and unfocused. The themes of evidence-based policy and joined-up government are highly relevant here – the ambitions are right but the current level of achievement is poor.

7.5.2 The knowledge base

The government potentially has a fantastic intelligence base, deploying all the capabilities of demographers, geographers and economists, for example. Analysis of this data provides the basis for articulating some of the major issues: for example, poverty and social exclusion, major migration flows, a growing elderly population needing appropriate pension support and health care. The government then has direct responsibility for the supply of major public services. It may be more accurate to describe these as major services to the public, because many of these are now supplied by private agencies, albeit under the umbrella of governmental purchase and regulation.

In each of the major areas – such as health, education, housing, transport, environmental impact, residential care for the elderly and crime – it is possible to enhance the information base by building system models, which (by analogy with the retail models discussed above) articulate needs and the ways in which these needs are met and could be met. In other words, the development of 'What if?' forecasting and planning is feasible and has been demonstrated in most areas.[9] However, this is rarely, if ever, done. There are enormous opportunities here.

A bonus from having adequate systems in place would be that good measures of performance would be available.[10]

In most cases, the production 'technologies' – hard and/or soft – are well understood. In some cases – medicine being the most obvious example – they are changing rapidly and there are associated problems of costs and budgeting.

7.5.3 Strategy

We work as usual with the BCW framework, though in this case the items, in the main, have to be interpreted differently. Although we are mainly concerned with public service, we should recognize at the outset that there is private provision in most cases for those who choose to pay, and there is often a private contribution to the public service.[11] Consider two examples: health and education. There are private hospitals and schools and, for such sectors, the strategic analysis is exactly as for a retailer – albeit selling a different kind of service. In the public sector, the managers of the services have to reinterpret *existing products to existing customers* and *new customers* in terms of estimating the demand for health and education services that have to be met. If all the demands cannot be met, then other parameters must change. In the health service, this might mean implicit rationing; in schools, higher class sizes than may be thought desirable.

Both sectors, particularly health, face questions of *new products and services* and *new delivery approaches*. Technical change in medicine is very dramatic (and expensive), for example. Delivery systems in education need to take new CIT systems into account, and particularly the internet as a new kind of 'library'. The *new geographies* question in this context is one concerning the changing geographical distribution of population. There is a serious issue, for example, of delivering GP services in inner-city areas as they become more polarized – and because the big hospitals are often in city centres, the tendency is to compensate by using A&E departments as a substitute for GP surgeries. There are questions of *industry structures* and *competition*. In the health case, these are matters of organization imposed by the government. And there is relatively little competition. Perhaps there ought to be! From a patient's perspective, the system is heavily regulated with even the choice of private treatment to an extent mediated through a nominated GP. In practice, there is relatively little freedom of choice in selecting GPs. In higher education, the system is different: there is genuine competition. In primary and secondary education, there is some competition but this is mediated mainly through the local authority management of catchment areas. This even has an impact on house prices as parents attempt to move into the catchment areas of 'good' schools. In the secondary education case, there is competition at the 16+ stage between school sixth forms, sixth form colleges and further education colleges.

The network size and shape questions posed for retailers can be posed again for health and education. The immediately relevant questions are the following: should the network consist of a small number of large branches or a large number of small ones? Should there be a hierarchy of branches? How does the network structure relate to hierarchical structure of service centres in cities and regions? The answers are more interesting than in the retail case. In the retail case, there is likely, in most cases, to be a uniform kind of answer dependent on the sector: for convenience goods, a network with a large number of small outlets; for supermarkets, a smaller number of larger outlets. In the health case, the provision varies from single doctor GP surgeries to large teaching hospitals with hundreds of beds and large A&E and outpatient departments. In the retail case, the network evolves in relation to the average distance consumers are prepared to travel for different kinds of goods and services. In the health case, it is necessary to balance the convenience of the patient with the ability to deliver specialist services: the more specialist the service, the fewer units there are likely to be nationally – and almost always located in large teaching hospitals. These tensions manifest themselves in public debate regularly, particularly when the closure of a small hospital is proposed. These delivery questions are particularly acute for, say, A&E services in sparsely populated rural areas.

In the schools' case, we can expect pupils to travel much shorter distances to primary schools than for secondary schools, and this will be reflected in the network structures and school sizes. The much harder questions are now those associated with social geography. There is a huge variation in achievement of pupils between, say, suburban and inner-city schools. This is partly a matter of what individual schools can achieve – because there will also be distributions around the average of achievement within a geographical category – and partly a matter of family support. (There may also be a 'hub and spokes' argument – as for hospitals.)

Against this background of well-informed intelligence, and, ideally, 'What if?' models, strategies can obviously be formulated. Delivery then depends critically on management and staffing and it is to these issues that we now turn.

7.5.4 Delivery: management structures and staffing

The health and education systems, in Mintzberg terms, are clearly professional bureaucracies. In other cases, like pensions, the system is a large administrative machine working according to the rules. In all cases, it is obviously necessary to have the appropriate set of skills and divisions of labour among the staff, functioning within an appropriate 'culture'. This last point is a difficult one. It is evident that the ambience of private hospitals or independent schools is 'better than' many public sector equivalents. Often, this is simply a matter of funding, but not always; the residual is culture.

Culture is in part a matter of 'loyalty' – and it may be that this is connected to a key management issue – the extent of devolution of authority. In health, for example, there is an attempt in the UK to run the *National* Health Service centrally, though this is now tempered by a move to give the large hospital trusts a greater degree of independence. Universities are interesting in this respect.

They have a lot of autonomy and it can be argued that they have succeeded, particularly in achieving and managing the growth in the last two decades, because of this. There are obvious lessons for the current debate in the UK on foundation hospitals.

In many public services, there are also important questions of 'joined-upness'. Consider the problems of crime. These are seen as issues for the police, the criminal justice system and the prison system. But they are also connected to education. Graduates, for example, do not (on the whole) commit crimes! But there are even more striking issues. A large proportion of young offenders in prison have been in 'care'. The child care system is clearly failing seriously. If this could be tackled, this might have one of the greatest impacts on crime levels. And this, in the main, is not being remedied by good educational facilities in prisons – notwithstanding some people trying very hard. Nor are there adequate mental health facilities in prisons and this is a serious issue since some significant percentage of the prison population, it can be argued, are there as a result of 'community' mental health provision itself being inadequate.

7.5.5 A special case for integration: city and regional planning

Cities and regions present a special kind of challenge for government. They are the theatres in which all the different kinds of activity come together. For any sector to thrive, for individuals to be able to lead rich lives, then cities and regions must thrive. All cities and regions are shaped by some degree of publicly provided infra-structure, particularly the transport networks. And they are to a greater or lesser extent planned and regulated at different scales. The challenge, therefore, is one of optimal planning – and the 'optimization' includes the 'amount' of planning as well as the plans and regulations themselves.

What we need to know about cities and regions can be structured in terms of:

* the population
    - where they live;
    - and work;
    - and from where public services are delivered;
* the economy
    - employment by sector;
    - the delivery of public services;
* and the infrastructure on which all these activities sit, including assessments of environmental impacts and sustainability.

The knowledge base is the information system that incorporates all this and a model system that represents the dynamics – the patterns of change. It would be possible to write lengthy essays on each of:

- migration;
- housing;
- public services;
- economic development, changing labour markets;
- infrastructure, environment, transport, increasing car ownership.

Cities and regions are complex mixtures of the private and the public, as we saw in Chapter 4. The task of the planner is to help optimize the allocation of public resources to facilitate the maintenance of 'good' towns and cities and for them to be able to develop effective futures for all of their populations. At present, this task seems to be largely beyond governments.

7.6 Concluding comment

What emerges from this account is that, while there is a much progress being made, in most cases organizations do not have what we have called requisite knowledge. And this means that, typically, they are not making the best use of available knowledge. There is a huge challenge to be met here and some options are explored in the concluding chapter.

Chapter 8

Knowledge power
A sea change?

8.1 What would constitute a sea change?

We have sought to generate a sketch map of what constitutes 'knowledge' and to show how this is changing over time. We have indicated what individuals and organizations have to do to acquire knowledge power and, in particular, to build requisite knowledge. But it is clear that the present structures of education and training, and, more broadly, the knowledge base of organizations, fall a long way short of the ideal. A sea change is needed. What would this be? We first summarize the book's conclusions to chart the sea change and then sketch what could be done in the next section. This provides the basis for suggesting the key action points for different players within the global knowledge system.

What would constitute a sea change?

- an education system that nurtured breadth and depth and that offered interdisciplinary perspectives at least as part of the 'breadth' but possibly also part of the 'depth';
- an approach to interdisciplinarity through a recognition that there are concepts that span traditional disciplines – the superconcepts;
- a recognition of the pace of knowledge development – the knowledge explosion – and what this means for lifelong learning;
- the provision of the facilities and incentives for lifelong learning;
- skills in employment that are being continually developed;
- an ability to tackle the biggest problems through research – the wicked issues.

8.2 How can a sea change be achieved?

When Tony Blair – at an early time in his premiership – was asked what his top three priorities were, he famously replied 'education, education and education'. In the long run, this analysis is at the root of any sea change. It is the education system that will deliver on a spectrum from a civilizing culture to the skills of employment, all in the context of lifelong learning. There will be difficult problems, as now, which come almost out of the blue, along with the long-standing wicked issues that remain a challenge, which means that a powerful research capability is also essential – a corollary of an effective education system. And these key ideas apply at all levels: the system, the school, college and university, and organizations –and they apply to each of us as individuals seeking to build the intellectual tool kit that allows us to be effective in a rapidly moving age.

If we take the generalized Cisco template in the form

{staff, what?, accountability, leadership} plus skills, how?, technology}

then we can take for granted that we need the best (educated and skilled) staff, and this includes 'leadership' at all levels; we can hope that systems of governance are in place which support 'accountability' without the downsides of crude performance management which lead to breakdowns of trust. We can assume that we will make the best use of technology, and indeed that we will develop new technology to con-tribute to problem-solving. The core of what is left is the 'what?' and the 'how?' and the challenges of 'breadth and depth'. The 'breadth and depth' argument runs through this book. We might summarize this key idea as: know something about everything, and everything about something. It is the 'knowing something about everything' that sows the seeds for identifying relevant superconcepts. The depth will usually come from one or two of the core disciplines, or a system of interest that spans a number of disciplines, in each case together with a knowledge of some enabling disciplines.

We examine these questions – first in education and then, in turn, for business and the public sector and for individuals. Each particular organization is part of a system – an ecosystem. We need to identify the key organizations within an eco-system that could be agents of change. In each case, we focus on education and training along with the implications for research.

In education, some of what should be taken for granted of course cannot be, in particular the universal supply of good teachers in all necessary subjects, and so these become urgent issues for policy makers. But these kinds of problems are at least well defined. It is much harder to tackle the 'curriculum and skills' issue. We begin with school education and illustrate the ecosystem idea with Figure 8.1. The argument is illustrated from the perpective of England (rather than the UK because education is devolved to Scotland, Wales and Northern Ireland). However, the argument can be translated in a straightforward way to other countries. This is an oversimplification, of course, but serves as an illustration. There are three layers: support, delivery and accountability. At the highest levels, there is central govern-ment as well as the various pressure groups and charitable foundations that have an interest. At the second support layer, it can be seen that university and col-lege schools of education play an important role in teacher supply and CPD and, though not mentioned explicitly in this layer, in pedagogy through their training of new teachers. Two government agencies are critical: the curriculum is established through the Qualifications and Curriculum Authority (QCA) and through the exam boards – the 'awarding bodies'; teacher supply (and much CPD) is driven by the Teacher Development Agency (TDA). There are players that function in both support layers – the learned societies, for example, sometimes combined through organizations such as SCORE[1] and ACME.[2] In the delivery layer, the 'networks and technology' box on the left supports the learning environment, which in turn supports both teachers and students. The outputs are measured and form the basis of a system of accountability that feeds back to the top layer.

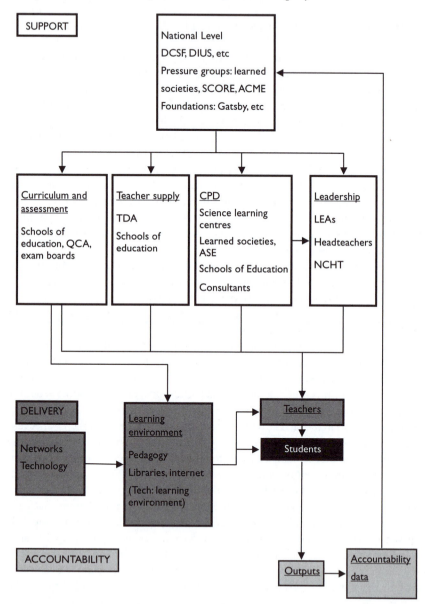

Figure 8.1 The education ecosystem.

The heart of the argument lies in the curriculum. This has been bedevilled by conflicting objectives: to provide an education for all – 'literacy' and 'numeracy' in the broadest senses – while at the same time, in the same schools and classrooms, providing stretch and challenge for the most able who might, for example, be the research scientists of the future. This presentation of the argument itself begs a number of questions, in particular, how the category of 'most able' is defined. Measured ability will relate to family background and culture. The challenge is to avoid accusations of elitism while meeting both objectives. The potential resolution is through our 'breadth and depth' argument: 'breadth' as a basis for all in a range of subjects, but with 'depth' being available at most ages. This in turn raises the question of the age at which it is desirable when there can be some degree of specialization.

What seems to have happened in England is that the key ecosystem players responsible for the curriculum have buried themselves in jargon that is impenetrable outside their own 'profession', possibly so to most teachers. This is then closely connected to assessment. This seems to have become very rigid. It is combined with a government principle that school improvement can be driven by publishing league tables of performance. The result of these two features in combination is that teachers 'teach to the test' and the wider benefits of education – indeed it can even be argued that the fundamentals of learning for students – are lost.

Viewed from outside the system, it seems that a solution should be achievable. It should be possible to sketch, at the highest levels, what constitutes the foundations of a discipline, or the knowledge of a system of interest that demands an interdisciplinary package of ideas and then to work backwards to answer the question: what would it be reasonable to know about that discipline or system at younger ages? In subjects with a reasonably linear development, such as mathematics, the progression should be straightforward. In all subjects, it should be possible to convey some of the excitement to come while teaching the foundations. It should be possible to offer breadth – from liberal arts and humanities to the ideas of science, along with the basics of numeracy and language – together with opportunities to pursue some subjects in depth.

More attention needs to be paid to the transition from school to university. At present, there is often a disjunction: the student turning up to read physics does not have the mathematical apparatus expected for the first year course, and so on. Most universities now recognize and deal with this through special classes. Ideally, it would be necessary to extend that idea and have foundation years, which would both offer the bases and associated enabling disciplines of subjects to be studied in depth as well as maintain an offering of breadth.

Universities are typically not restricted to a national curriculum. This provides a rich diversity of institutions and overcomes the school difficulty of the conflicting objectives of 'literacy' versus 'stretch and challenge'. There will be a variety of courses across the system to meet all kinds of needs. However, as we have hinted in Chapter 6, there is possibly a price to be paid in inefficiency here.

The argument then extends very importantly into lifelong learning. The 'curriculum' argument – the 'what?' – is essentially the same except that more of it is likely to be vocational. The 'how?' is very much more complicated because there are so many institutions that can function as providers. There is a multitude of qualifications into the bargain, though that may be seen as a rich diversity meeting a corresponding diversity of needs.

In the case of business, we have seen that what is needed is the maintenance and development of requisite knowledge in relation to the template of Chapter 5. Companies are implicitly aware of this as shown through recognition of the importance of training and, in many cases, of the formal introduction of 'knowledge management'.

In the case of government and public services, the 'requisite knowledge' argument is shared with business – it is a requirement for all kinds of organizations but the success criteria are different. The argument is complicated here because of the relative role distinctions between different players: politicians, special advisers, civil servants, chief scientific advisers and the different 'analysis' professions – economists, statisticians, scientists, operational researchers, social researchers. It is not easy to combine their different knowledge bases into one package of 'requisite' knowledge – but that is the challenge.

8.3 Individuals: building an intellectual tool kit

Individual responsibility for engaging with the knowledge power agenda is paramount. We all have an intellectual tool kit, whether consciously or not. It is the basis of how we think, how we approach problems. We all need to refine it continuously – as one approach to lifelong learning. There are particular needs of:

- sixth formers deciding what to read at university;
- undergraduates needing a wider context for their studies, needing to apply their imagination to the idea of superconcepts in their own thinking;
- employees – again to understand context, to be capable problem solvers, able to think outside the box; to understand their own organization – how they can contribute, how it might change;
- managers and strategists;
- public policy makers and politicians.

It may seem odd at first sight to cover such a span of experience but, put simply, knowledge power is enhanced by lifelong learning – and lifelong learning begins early, and is lifelong! In this concluding chapter, therefore, we draw the threads together of the argument to provide a framework for the continuing development of an intellectual tool kit. The key elements are:

- breadth and depth – recall the '10,000 hours' argument on depth – the time needed to be really good at something;

- the 'breadth', which also provides the basis for being flexible and tolerant;
- building a personal vocabulary of superconcepts;
- adopting a systems perspective;
- knowing something about the structures of organizations;
- being intellectually ambitious and being prepared to take on 'wicked' problems;
- searching for requisite knowledge in relation to any issue associated with the system of interest;
- being committed to lifelong learning.

The main aim of the book has been to provide the illustrations that will facilitate the building of the tool kit!

The power of mathematics

A1.1 Introduction

Many people fear mathematics. The aim of this Appendix is to demonstrate that without any serious mathematical background, it is possible to be introduced to the power of mathematics for describing complex systems in an economical way. This then opens up the route to some deep insights on the evolution of complex systems. To fix ideas, we consider the retail centres of London – 220 of them – and the pattern of trips to them from residential wards – 623 of these. A map is

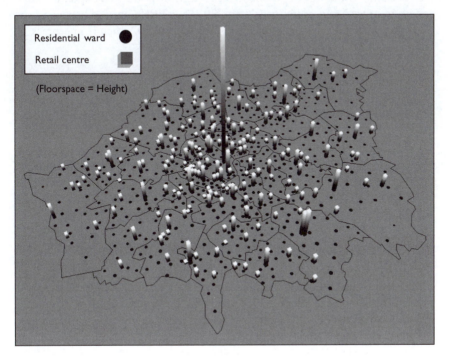

Figure A1.1 Residential wards and retail centres in London.

shown in Figure A1.1.

We first demonstrate the power of description (section A1.2) and then we extend this so that we can build a model (section A1.3). Finally, we show how the system acts as a demonstrator of some of the main features of complexity science (A1.4–A1.6).

A1.2 Mathematics as a powerful descriptor

Consider the following task: to find a way of representing all the flows – from each residential zone to each retail centre. There are 623×220 possible interactions, which is 137,060, a relatively large number. Consider just one of these. Figure A1.2 repeats the map but identifies one residential zone and one retail centre – say, Hampstead and the West End respectively. Suppose we measure the flow in money units and determine that, on average, this flow is £1050 units per day (measured in thousands). We can then label this and record the volume as

$$S_{\text{Hampstead, West end}} = 1050 \tag{1}$$

We now proceed through two levels of abstraction. First, suppose we number all the residential zones from 1 to 623, instead of their having geographical names, and we number retail centres from 1 to 220. Then, if Hampstead happens to be residential zone 124 and the West End is retail centre 102, then (1) becomes

$$S_{220,124} = 1050 \tag{2}$$

We can then in principle write out all 137,060 flows systematically, starting with a row for all the flows leaving residential zone, 1, then zone 2, and so on:

$$S_{1,1} \; S_{1,2} \; S_{1,3} \; S_{1,4} \ldots\ldots\ldots\ldots\ldots\ldots\ldots S_{1,124}$$

$$S_{2,1} \; S_{2,2} \; S_{2,3} \; S_{2,4} \ldots\ldots\ldots\ldots\ldots\ldots\ldots S_{2,124}$$

$$\ldots\ldots\ldots\ldots\ldots\ldots\ldots\ldots\ldots\ldots\ldots\ldots\ldots \tag{3}$$

$$S_{623,1} \; S_{623,2} \; S_{623,3} \; S_{623,4} \ldots\ldots\ldots\ldots S_{623,124}$$

This array has the form of a set of accounts. The elements of each row total up all the flows leaving a zone, and the elements of a column sum to all the flows entering a retain centre. Figure A1.2 shows the Hampstead Town ward and the West End retail centre.

Figure A1.3 shows the flows.

The next level of abstraction is to label any residential zone with a letter, say i; and similarly any retail centre, say j. Then (2) becomes

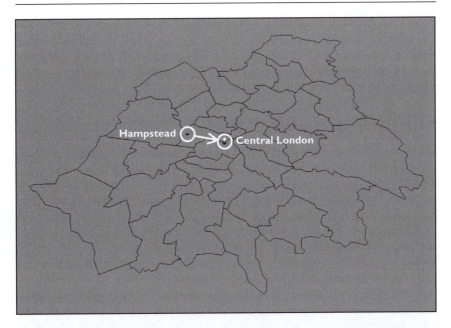

Figure A1.2 Hampstead Town residential ward and central London retail centre.

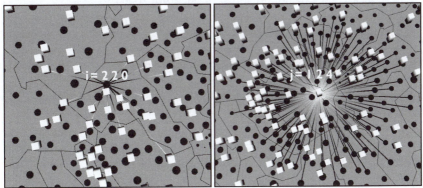

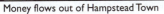   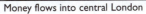

Money flows out of Hampstead Town   Money flows into central London

Figure A1.3 Flows out of Hampstead Town and into central London.

$$S_{i,\,j} = 1050, i = 220, j = 124 \tag{4}$$

Mathematicians have invented a notation so that a single letter can represent the whole array (3), or, probably more helpfully, show the index:

$$S = \{S_{ij}\}, i = 1, 623, j = 1, 220 \tag{5}$$

(When a single letter is used to denote an array, it is usually shown in bold – or, especially in manuscript, underlined.) Hence, the array (3) with its large number of elements can be represented very economically as (5). And, of course, computers can store this kind of information very easily. This is achieved by allowing ourselves to talk about *any* zone i, and *any* zone j.

A1.3 Building a model

The beauty of the level of abstraction that has been achieved is that we can now seek to build a model, in this case an equation for S_{ij}, which we can write in the form

$$S_{ij} = \text{.....................................} \qquad (6)$$

and because this holds for each i = 1, 2, 3, ... 623 and each j = 1, 2, 3, ... 220 = that is, for each element of the array (3) above – this means that in one line, we can represent 137,060 equations.

To build the model, we need to define some more variables – system descriptors. Consider any residential zone, i, and any retail centre, j, and define the following:

e_i = the average expenditure for the residents of zone i;

P_i = the population of the zone;

W_j = the size (in floorspace) of the retail centre in j;

c_{ij} = the cost of travel between i and j.

Then a really simple model would be

$$S_{ij} = Ke_iP_iW_j/c_{ij} \qquad (7)$$

That is, the flow, in money units, is proportional to the total cash available for retail in zone i, the size of zone j, and is inversely proportional to the distance between them. It turns out that we have to do something more sophisticated and replace the constant, K, by a set of constants, A_i, that is make the constant zone dependent, and instead of having an inverse *linear* relationship in travel cost, we introduce a decreasing function of c_{ij}, which we call $f(c_{ij})$. Equation (7) then becomes

$$S_{ij} = A_ie_iP_iW_jf(c_{ij}) \qquad (8)$$

If, for example,

$$f(c_{ij}) = 1/c_{ij}^2 = c_{ij}^{-2} \tag{9}$$

which would be an inverse square law, then (7) would represent a kind of 'gravity model' with the flow, the interaction, proportional to each of the two masses ($e_i P_i$ and W_j) and inversely proportional to the square of the travel cost between them.

Equation (7) is near to being a plausible model. The computer would make light work of the implied 137,060 calculations to produce each element of the array (3).

We noted in relation to the array (3) that the row elements summed to all the flows leaving a zone and the column elements to all those arriving at the destination. These are shown symbolically in Figure A1.3. and in equation form below:

$$S_{i1} + S_{i2} + S_{i3} + \dots\dots\dots\dots\dots\dots = e_i P_i \tag{10}$$

$$S_{1j} + S_{2j} + S_{3j} + \dots\dots\dots\dots\dots\dots = D_j \tag{11}$$

noting that the row sums must add up to $e_i P_i$. For the column sums, we have introduced the term D_j, which would be the total revenue attracted into j. We can then introduce the sigma notation for a sum, and the right hand sides of (10) and (11) can be denoted as follows

$$S_{i1} + S_{i2} + S_{i3} + \dots\dots\dots\dots\dots\dots = \Sigma_j S_{ij} \tag{12}$$

$$S_{1j} + S_{2j} + S_{3j} + \dots\dots\dots\dots\dots\dots = \Sigma_i S_{IJ} \tag{13}$$

where Σ_j stands for 'sum over j' and Σ_i stands for 'sum over i'.

The final step in building the model is to introduce two parameters. First, we can interpret W_j as the pulling power – the 'attractiveness' – of the shopping centre at zone j and to raise it to a power – a parameter that will indicate how important size is in this respect. So W_j will become W_j^α in the model. The greater α, the more important 'size' is to the consumer – through choice, economies of scale and so on. Second, we can make the function $f(c_{ij})$ explicit in a way that introduces a parameter that determines how far people travel on average. This could be done by replacing c_{ij}^{-2} in (9) by $c_{ij}^{-\beta}$. Then, if β is large, trips will be relatively short, and vice versa. However, it is more customary to use a negative exponential function than a power function, which we will write as $\exp(-\beta c_{ij})$. We can also be explicit about the A_i term in equation (8). It is calculated to ensure that all the money is spent! That is, to ensure that

$$\Sigma_j S_{ij} = e_i P_i \tag{14}$$

the model then becomes

$$S_{ij} = A_i e_i P_i W_j^\alpha exp(-\beta c_{ij}) \tag{15}$$

where

$$A_i = \Sigma_k W_k^\alpha exp(-\beta c_{ik}) \tag{16}$$

If these last steps are difficult, this should not be a cause for too much concern. The principles invoked to reach the primitive form of model in equations (8) and (9) are the same. The refinements make the model realistic and give us two parameters, α and β, which enable us to use the model to describe different kinds of retail systems.

A1.4 Running the model

The equations (15) and (16) can be coded as a computer model so that, given the inputs, we can calculate the flows $\{S_{ij}\}$. Note then that we can calculate the column sums of the array. We introduced D_j earlier as the total revenue flowing into a retail centre. We can now see that, using the sigma notation

$$D_j = \Sigma_i S_{ij} \tag{17}$$

The importance of this is that it gives us 'flight simulator' capabilities. If a retail centre is to be expanded through a proposed new development, for example, this can be represented in the model by changing the appropriate W_j. The model can be re-run, the new array $\{S_{ij}\}$ calculated, and the revenue into the new centre, D_j calculated, and the impact on all the other centres – the trade that is taken away from these by the expansion of one centre – is also available.

For example, see Figure A1.4, which shows the London landscape of Figure A1.1 with the new Westfield shopping centre added. The model can be run to calculate the total revenue attracted to the new centre and, just as importantly in some instances, where this revenue has been attracted from.

We should also note that this kind of model is applicable to any interaction within cities: trips to schools or hospitals, for example, and again the simulator capability is potentially invaluable. The model can, of course, be further refined. It can be disaggregated to represent different kinds of retail goods. It could then be re-aggregated to model flows into retail centres, or it could be run for a single group such as 'food'. In this latter case, we should note that supermarket companies routinely use this kind of model to plan the optimum location of their stores.

A1.5 Dynamics

The next step is to ask the more challenging question: how does the retail structure of the city evolve over time? This structure is represented by $\{W_1, W_2, W_3, ...\}$, which can now be written in an obvious compact notation as $\{W_j\}$. We work out

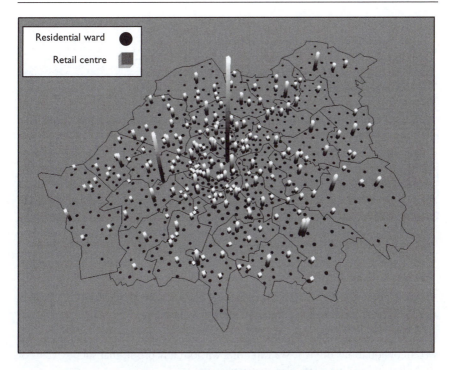

Figure A1.4 London with the Westfield shopping centre added.

how to represent a simple hypothesis: that a particular centre will grow if it is currently profitable and will decline if not. Suppose Wj is measured by floorspace. We then let K be the (annual, say) cost of running the centre per unit, so KW_j is the total cost. We know the revenue attracted is Dj and so the profit (or loss) is

$$D_j - KW_j \qquad (18)$$

We then introduce one new piece of notation: we use the symbol 'Δ' to represent 'change in' so that ΔW_j can be the change in W_j in a year, say. Then our hypothesis can be written

$$\Delta W_j = \varepsilon[D_j - KW_j] \qquad (19)$$

and, again, this can be programmed into the computer. The step can be repeated for a number of time periods and hence we can simulate the dynamics – the evolution of spatial structure. A timeline is shown in Figure A1.5.

If we think the system is such that it achieves equilibrium, then the resulting structure arises when

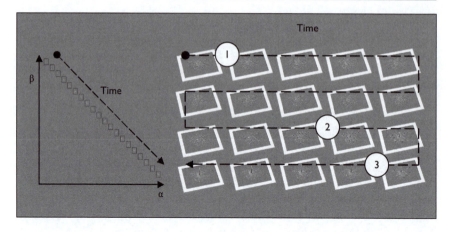

Figure A1.5 A diagonal slice through the **(α, β)** grid illustrating a hypothetical timeline.

$$\Delta W_j = \varepsilon[D_j - KW_j] = 0 \tag{20}$$

A1.6 Illustrations of complexity science

Even a cursory study of equations (15), (16) and (19) show that this is a nonlinear system of equations in $\{W_j\}$. We can note, without any proof, that such systems of equations have some particular properties:

- they have multiple equilibria;
- the solutions are very dependent on the initial conditions;
- there can be abrupt changes – phase transitions – at critical points.

The demonstration retail model in this Appendix demonstrates all of these properties and illustrates many of the key features of complexity science. The first of these points is essentially technical for present purposes, but underpins the second. Consider Figure A1.5 above: each step in time offers new 'initial conditions' for the next step, and this is the notion of 'path dependence' we introduced as a superconcept in the main text. Similarly, we introduced 'phase transition' as a superconcept. The introduction of a new shopping centre, like Westfield in the illustration above, would be a major change in initial conditions and hence the path. The classic example of a major phase transition occurred in the late 1950s and early 1960s when there was a shift from 'corner shop' food retailing to supermarkets – a transition brought about by increasing car ownership and a corresponding increase in ease of travel.

The challenge for planners operating in the context of complexity is to be able to identify possible phase transitions and to either steer towards them if they are desirable – or vice versa.

Superconcepts

1 C-societies
   1a: cognitive
   1b: creative
   1c: communications
2 The Cisco template:
   {reform (teacher quality, curriculum, accountability, leadership), skills, pedagogy, technology}
3 Accountability
4 Curriculum
5 Leadership
6 Pedagogy
7 Skills
8 Technology
9 The consensus theory of truth
10 The deductive/inductive, mathematics/statistics distinction
11 Beyond the linear – wikis and multidimensional classification
12 Systems of interest
13 Scale
14 Simplification: simplify the picture of the system of interest as much as possible to get to the essence of any 'law'
15 Energy
16 Field (of force)
17 Interaction
18 Conservation laws
19 Entropy
20 (Boltzmann) statistical averaging as a means of simplification
21 Phase transitions – sudden changes in structure at critical points
22 The uncertainty principle
23 DNA as information carrier and development controller
24 Hierarchical systems
25 Evolution
26 Principles of evolution – e.g. the survival of the fittest

27 Trophic levels
28 Food chains
29 Prey–predator interactions
30 Competition for resources
31 Utility function and profit maximization
32 Input–output model
33 Rent and land value
34 Evidence-based knowledge
35 Policy, design and analysis: three ways of thinking
36 System
37 System representation
38 Location
39 Accounts
40 Complexity
41 Disorganized complexity
42 Organized complexity
43 Information
44 Variety
45 Requisite variety
46 Control
47 (System) model
48 Theory
49 Understanding
50 Explanation
51 (Flight) simulators
52 Structuralism
53 Optimization
54 Constraints, as representing system knowledge
55 Pattern recognition
56 Combinatorics
57 Multiple equilibria
58 Path dependence
59 Location, nodes
60 Function
61 Structure
62 Performance indicators
63 Organizational efficiency
64 Catchment populations
65 Effective delivery
66 Networks
67 Shortest path in a network
68 Fast and slow dynamics
69 Equilibrium
70 Nonlinear systems

71 Critical points
72 Initial conditions
73 Emergence
74 Prey–predator model
75 Competition-for-resources model
76 Periodic solutions
77 Chaos theory
78 The production 'technology'
79 The market (or client base)
80 The business environment
81 Strategy
82 Delivery – management structures and skills
83 Quality at an appropriate price
84 Monopolistic benefits
85 Mintzberg's organization types
   a. simple
   b. machine
   c. professional bureaucracy
   d. divisional
   e. adhocracy
86 Central nervous system (VSM) structures
87 The 'war room'
88 The business excellence model
89 Complexity theory
90 General systems theory
91 Cybernetics
92 Control systems
93 Computer models
94 Computer visualization
95 Microsimulation
96 Computer algorithms
97 Graphical models
98 Intelligent search
99 Neural networks
100 Adaptive systems
101 Christensen units
102 Planning horizons
103 Ambidextrous organizations – short-run efficiency and long-run innovation

Glossary of superconcepts

This aims to provide a guide to some of the main concepts introduced in the text. It can be used to recap or – because the concepts below are interlinked through the use of 'q.v.' (meaning 'quod vide' – 'see this') – to relate one particular concept to others. They are presented here is alphabetical order, rather than the text order in the list in Appendix 2, except for the first entry which recurs so often later that it is offered up front. Some additional terms have been added to help in constructing appropriate definitions and to make the glossary self-contained.

System of interest   This is a phrase perhaps most commonly used by physicists in wanting to focus on a particular system to make a particular point. However, it is powerful in general in two respects: first, it ensures that we think in 'systems' terms, emphasizing interconnectedness and complexity; second, it forces us to be specific in particular instances in defining what we are thinking about. This is not restrictive – a system of interest can be connected to other systems of interest and so on.

Accountability   Organizations usually have to be accountable to someone or somebody: companies to shareholders and clients and customers, government and public sector organizations first to a governing body and second to a wider community of stakeholders.

Accounts   Systems are made up of elements of different types. It is usually important to count these – money in a financial system, people in a demographic system. It is then useful to track these counts over time and to understand the processes of change – profit and loss or birth, death and migration.

Adaptive systems   A particular subclass of complex systems is the set of so-called adaptive systems. These can change as a result of environmental interactions or through the modification of **DNA** (q.v.) (or equivalents) in an **evolutionary** (q.v.) process.

Ambidextrous organizations   These are organizations that are capable of managing their core businesses successfully in the short run but can also innovate for the longer run.

Ashby's law of requisite variety   See **requisite variety** (q.v.).

Beer's *Brain of the firm* model   Stafford Beer published his book *Brain of the firm* in 1972. It examined the structure of the **central nervous system** (q.v.) as a model for other sophisticated viable systems [**VSM** (q.v.)]

Boltzmann   Ludwig Boltzmann is recognized as one of the founders of **statistical mechanics** (q.v.) in physics in the late nineteenth century. It was a theory of gases and was an atomic or molecular theory – in that respect, ahead of its time. The key idea was that, while it was impossible to chart the movement of each molecule of a gas on the basis of Newton's laws of motion – there being of the order of 10^{23} simultaneous equations to solve – it was also possible to use a statistical averaging procedure to deduce the macro properties of the gas. He was able to use the methods of **combinatorics** (q.v.) and the idea of **variety** (q.v.) (though he did not call it that) to show that of all the possible states of the system, at the macrolevel, one was overwhelmingly the most probable. The procedure involved maximizing an **entropy** (q.v.) function. It was only in the mid-twentieth century that it was realized by a number of authors that this was a principle that could be applied in a wide variety of situations in many disciplines.

Business environment   Any business, like any **system** (q.v.) functions in an **environment** (q.v.) and managers and leaders need to have their own models of this.

Business excellence model   This was developed by John Oakland (see bibliography).

Catchment population   A school, a hospital or a shopping centre draw pupils, patients or customers from a catchment area. It is quite common to attempt to draw catchments in such a way that the do not overlap – but in real life they do overlap and hence the need for **spatial interaction models** (q.v.).

Central nervous system (VSM) structures   Stafford Beer argued in his book *Brain of the firm* that the most successful **control system** (q.v.) ever to have evolved in nature is the human brain and it would, therefore, be interesting to examine its structure to see what could be learned about **management structures** (q.v.) in organizations. He identified five levels – the top concerned with **strategy** (q.v.), the bottom three, in effect, with implementation, but a level 4 that was about information filtering. He observed that very few organizations had a 'level 4' but cited the cabinet '**war room**' (q.v.) in England in World War II as an example. He generalized the idea to the **VSM** (q.v.) – 'viable system model' – concept in later books.

Chaos theory   In some models – for example, the **Lotka-Volterra model** (q.v.) (as first pointed out by Robert May), an increase in the response parameter will lead first to regular periodic behaviour, but then to oscillations which show no regular pattern of any kind and are described as chaotic. There is an undoubted mathematical interest in these solutions and some may occur naturally in areas like climatology. However, in most economic and social systems, in reality, the response in relation to structural change is likely to be much smaller and inertia on the ground inhibits oscillatory or chaotic behaviour.

Christensen units   Clayton Christensen identified the idea of 'disruptive technologies' – new technologies that are needed to be competitive but which are
disrupted by existing staff. His solution to the disruption is to introduce the
new technologies into new units alongside the old ones, possibly with new
staff. If they succeed, they will take over.

Cisco template   Cisco's Global Education Group produced a White Paper
in 2008 titled *Equipping every learner for the 21st Century*. It likened contemporary reforms of education systems to the development of Web 2.0
and characterized these by emphases on teacher quality, good curriculum,
accountability and leadership. It then identified the addition of twenty-first
century **skills** (q.v.), newer **pedagogies** (q.v.) and the application of technology as drivers from education 2.0 to what has been dubbed 3.0.

Combinatorics   How many ways are there of selecting a team of 11 football
players from a squad of 22? The answer is $22!/11!11!$, which is $705,432$ – a
very large number.[1] Many choices faced by managers and policy makers are
of this kind. It becomes important to find optimum – or simply, 'good',
'satisficing'[2] solutions. The 'number of possible states of a system' is also a
combinatorial issue and the mathematics of this underpins the notions of
variety (q.v.) and **Boltzmann**'s (q.v.) approach to **entropy** (q.v.) – which can
then be generalized in interesting ways.[3]

Competition for resources model   This is a version of the **Lotka-Volterra**
model (q.v.) but rather than modelling prey and predator species, this represents a number of species competing for resources. It has many applications
beyond the confines of ecology.

Complex systems theory   See **complexity** (q.v.). The idea of complex systems
theory is a contemporary version of **general systems theory** (q.v.)

Complexity   The 'complexity' concept is at the heart of the new science – 'complexity science'. Weaver's distinction is an important one:
(9a) Simple systems are those with relatively few elements and 'handle-able'
    interactions.
Complex systems have many elements and complex interaction structures and
Weaver identified two main types:
(9b) Disorganized systems – with large numbers of elements but where
    the interactions are relatively weak.
(9c) Organized systems – again large numbers of elements but at least some
    of them strongly connected with others.
Essentially, the methods of **Boltzmann** (q.v.) can be used to understand
systems of disorganized complexity, but systems of organized complexity are
of greater **variety** (q.v.) and more challenging.

Computer algorithms   Mathematical **models** (q.v.) are essentially built algebraically from sets of simultaneous equations. Computers have in effect offered
an extension of this kind of mathematics by providing the means for solving
certain kinds of problems through computer algorithms – computational
schemes that cannot be written down as equations in the usual way. A good

example is the calculation of the set of **shortest paths in a network** (q.v.). These algorithms become key components of **computer models** (q.v.).

Computer models   A **model** (q.v.) is a formal representation of a system of interest. A computer model is such a representation on a computer. The power of modern computers is such that increasingly complex systems can be so represented and used as the basis of computer simulation and 'What if?' exploration.

Computer visualization   One of the substantial achievements of the development of computer technology has been in the field of computer graphics. This is particularly important in the analysis of **computer models** (q.v.) of **nonlinear** (q.v.) **complex** (q.v.) systems. Such models are made up of sets of equations that cannot be solved analytically but whose solutions can be calculated numerically on the computer and then visualized through computer graphics.

Consensus theory of truth   Jurgen Habermas has argued that what is true is what we can easily agree about – given effective intersubjective communication. This view has the advantage that it shows that while it is easy to establish something called 'truth' in the sciences, it is much more difficult in social and political fields.

Conservation principles   There are often important elements of systems that are conserved. Sometimes this leads to formal laws, such as the 'conservation of energy' in physics. In other cases, it is not given the status of a law but is nonetheless important. We do not speak of the 'conservation of money' but what accountants do is essentially set up a framework that is underpinned by just that. It is particularly important to take note of conservation properties in model building. These represent much of our knowledge of the system of interest, which can be represented in **constraint** (q.v.) equations and, of course, they relate to a broader conception of **accounts** (q.v.) than financial accounts.

Constraints   Constraints can contain much of our knowledge about a system. **Conservation principles** (q.v.) can be represented as constraints on the possible vales of variables in model development. For example, if the journey to work is being modelled, then the total at the resident end must relate to the number of workers there, and similarly at the employment end.

Control theory   Systems often have to be controlled. The driver of the car controls the car for example. Control theory is about designing control systems, usually in machines, but in superconcept terms it can be deployed more widely – as in **Ashby's Law of requisite variety** (q.v.).

Critical parameter   A **model** (q.v.) has parameters – for example in the transport case, representing ease of travel. A **phase change** (q.v.) can occur when a parameter takes a critical value.

Critical points   These are the points in time in the evolution of a system of interest that is **nonlinear** (q.v.) at which there is some abrupt change in structure – a **phase change** (q.v.).

C-societies and organizations, with the following capabilities:
- (1a) cognitive
- (1b) creative
- (1c) communications

This provides a framework for assessing whether societies – or organizations – have the capacities to be successful. The 'cognitive' is about the knowledge base – closely related to **'requisite knowledge'** (q.v.). The knowledge base, and hence creativity, has to grow. And it has to be communicated – as in teaching – but also plays a role as the basis of the **'consensus theory of truth'** (q.v).

Curriculum   Traditionally, a curriculum is what is taught in education – in schools, colleges and universities. In this book, we have broadened its use to 'What we do' and 'What we need to know' for different kinds of organizations. Put briefly, the 'What' [the organization is about].

Cybernetics   From the Greek 'steersman' – it grew up in the 1960s as the 'science of control' – this with strong engineering connotations. It has not taken off in a major way possibly because it was in competition with **operational research** (q.v.), control engineering, and developing branches of mathematics in control theory.

Deductive/inductive, mathematics/statistics distinction   Philosophers of science make a distinction between the hypothetico-deductive method for building **theories** (q.v.) for testing and the inductive method – inferring theories and laws from the data. This relates closely to the difference between mathematics and statistics and the way in which the practitioners of these two disciplines approach research. In economics, for example, it is the difference in approach between mathematical economics on the one hand and econometrics on the other. It is important to understand these differences in interpreting research.

Delivery   For an organization to have the capacity to deliver its **strategy** (q.v.), it will need appropriate management structures and **skills** (q.v.)

Differential or **difference equations**   These are the mathematical equations in a **model** (q.v.) which represent change over time. In differential equations, time is treated continuously; in difference equations, discretely.

DNA   DNA – deoxyribonucleic acid – is a nucleic acid whose structure was famously discovered by Crick and Watson in the 1950s and which is the basis of genes. It controls the replication of cells, the development of organisms and is the basis of inheritance.

Effective delivery   **Performance indicators** (q.v.) normally relate to the efficiency and effectiveness of an institution. It is also possible to reverse the interaction between institution and customer/client and ask whether a service (for example) is being effectively delivered to that person or group. It is likely, for example in the UK, that dental surgeries are efficient but that dental services are not being delivered comprehensively to the population.

Emergence   At **critical points** (q.v.), a system's **structure** (q.v.) can change abruptly – a **phase change** (q.v.). It is particularly interesting when a completely new and hitherto unanticipated structure appears. This phenomenon has been characterized as 'emergence'.

Energy   Energy plays a critical role in physics, for example in the laws of thermodynamics. When the methods of statistical mechanics – as **statistical averaging** (q.v) – are applied in other fields, it is always interesting to explore what the analogies of 'energy' are.

Entropy   This is a subtle concept that has been defined in different ways in different contexts but with an underlying common meaning. It is the basis of statistical averaging procedures that are very important for building certain kinds of **computer model** (q.v.). It was fully developed by **Boltzmann** (q.v.) in the context of the physics of gases at the end of the nineteenth century but more recently has been applied much more widely.

Environment   A **system** (q.v.) is only likely to be isolated as a theoretical construct. Physicists, for example, often describe isolated systems to explore the effects of particular laws. It is a way of keeping everything else 'constant'. In reality, a system of interest is located in an environment and it is necessary to articulate the interactions between the system and its environment. Of course the term is used more broadly and colloquially to represent Earth's environment or, in practice, some part of that.

Equilibrium   The classical illustration of an equilibrium in physics is a ball at the bottom of an hemispherical bowl. If it is disturbed, then albeit after a few oscillations, it will return to the bottom of the bowl – a stable equilibrium. If the bowl was turned upside down and the ball was somehow perched on top, then if it was disturbed, it would fall off – an unstable equilibrium. Many more complex systems of interest have equilibrium states. Sometimes, as they change through time, they never achieve equilibrium but can still be considered as governed by an underlying (possibly itself continually changing) equilibrium.

Evolution   'Evolution' has both a colloquial use and several possible technical uses. As any system of interest changes over time, it can be said to evolve. More specifically, it may be appropriate to articulate the theory of evolution in a particular case. The most famous case is that of Charles Darwin in *The origin of species* where the theory is rooted in the idea of 'the survival of the fittest'.

Explanation   See **understanding** (q.v.).

Facts   There is a simple way of thinking that asserts that what is true is a fact and vice versa. However, '**understanding**' (q.v.) is more complicated than that. Beyond facts that are almost (or actually) tautologies, such as $1+1 = 2$, there is nearly always a provisional nature about what is true.

Fast dynamics   For change processes, after a disturbance, a system can return to an **equilibrium** (q.v.) very quickly – and this is known as fast dynamics. Other systems return only slowly – **slow dynamics**. For many systems of interest, there are subsystems that are of the fast dynamics type and other subsystems – perhaps associated with **structures** (q.v.) – governed by slow dynamics.

Field (of force)   The best known fields are those in physics: gravitational, magnetic or electrical fields. However, it is sometimes useful to think of fields in other contexts – for example the rent gradients across a city.

Flight simulators   When pilots are trained, simulators are used. They sit at the controls of an 'aircraft', which is actually a computer model, with a screen in front of them which gives a realistic view of what they are achieving piloting the craft in different circumstances. This kind of 'What if?' simulator can be used in a much wider variety of circumstances. Computer models can be built to represent systems of interest and managers and planners can explore 'What if?' simulations of possible futures.

Flows   Interactions (q.v.) often manifest themselves as flows: nutrients round an ecosystem, people travelling for various purposes and so on.

Function   'Function' can be used in its colloquial sense – as describing the role of a system or an element of a system – or its more technical mathematical use. The latter shows how a dependent variable is a function of one or more independent variables.

General systems theory   The idea of a general systems theory is usually associated with the work of Ludwig von Bertalanffy in the 1950s. It is a response to the question: is it possible to have a general theory of any system? In a sense, is it possible to rise above disciplines? It remains a noble idea that essentially failed at the time but is in one sense being resurrected as **complex systems theory** (q.v.).

Graphical models   There is a scheme of formal model building that involves articulating diagrams representing the structure of a system of interest, which then provides the basis for writing down the corresponding algebraic equations.

Hierarchy   There are many obvious hierarchies in the structures we observe in everyday life: a tree with a trunk, main branches, subsidiary branches and so on; a road network with motorways, arterial main roads, minor roads and by-ways. These are important features of system definition and systems of interest need to be understood at different levels in the hierarchy. There will be interactions between different levels of the hierarchy.

Information   'Information' has a range of colloquial meanings that actually serve us well. It is the 'data' that underpins 'knowledge' – qualitative or quantitative. It is used more formally in telecommunications and computer science where measures are needed to quantify the flow of digital information in networks. This measure – an **entropy** (q.v.) measure – was developed by Claude Shannon and reported in the book by Shannon and Weaver (1945).

Initial conditions   A mathematical or computer dynamic **model** (q.v.) is represented by a set of **differential or difference equations** (q.v.). The solutions to these equations at a point in time are dependent on the initial values of the variables at an earlier time – the 'initial conditions'. This is the basis of **path dependence** (q.v.).

Intelligent search   As massive information systems become available – such as Google, Wikipedia and many more – the issue of intelligent search becomes critically important. It has implications for education when these instruments are used as tools by students and it has implications for research because, as search tools, these systems become the new library.

Interaction   Systems are interesting because their elements interact and so charting out interaction patterns is very important. Spatial interaction is particularly important, for example the 'journey to work' in cities charts the relationship between homes and workplaces. There are **computer models** (q.v.) of these interaction patterns that can be built using **statistical averaging** (q.v.), that is, **Boltzmann's** (q.v.) **entropy** (q.v.) – maximizing principles.

Leadership   This is an elusive concept. The chief executive of an organization clearly has to be a leader with his or her senior management team and indeed the wider organization. But there is a sense in which 'management' is for everybody and therefore there are many leadership opportunities that are not always recognized as such.

Location   There are many problems where spatial structure is important and entities within a system, for example, will be characterized in part by location. **Interaction** (q.v.) might then be represented as the **flows** (q.v.) between locations. It is also important to recognize a **hierarchy** (q.v.) of locations: say national, regional and local in geographical terms. It may then be important to beware of national policies, which need to be applied differently at local levels to reflect local needs and variations.

Lotka-Volterra model   Lotka and Volterra were the two scientists who (independently) discovered the **prey–predator** (q.v.) and the **competition for resources models** (q.v.), which underpin much of ecology and have elided into other disciplines.

Management structures and skills   Organizations will be managed and, implicitly or explicitly, have a management structure, staffed by people with appropriate skills. It is worth thinking the associated issues through explicitly. **Mintzberg** (q.v.) provides an appropriate starting point.

Market (or client base)   A 'market' is a shorthand for a set of consumers competing to purchase goods or a service. There are many economic (and political) models of markets. In the case of public services, there is an obvious extension of the definition, with the 'market' idea correspondingly broadened.

Mathematical programming   This is the name given to the branch of mathematics concerned with **optimization** (q.v.).

Microsimulation   Microsimulation involves building a **computer model** (q.v.) that generates a representation of a real population on the machine: that is, a population of individuals whose characteristics closely resemble those of a real population.

Mintzberg's organization types   Considerable insight can be gained on **management structures** (q.v.) by a study of Mintzberg's organization types. He discusses what he calls 'types of bureaucracies'. He distinguished simple, machine, divisional and professional bureaucracies, and what he called an adhocracy. 'Simple' might describe a small family firm for example; 'machine', a structure that is very rules driven; 'divisional', the kind of structure that can arise as a simple system bifurcates. The idea of a professional bureaucracy is a very interesting one – universities or hospitals are examples – because Mintzberg identifies them through their front-line workers being top-class professionals and argues that such people would expect to be involved with the management. An adhocracy is a much looser structure – such as a management consultancy that is constantly forming temporary project groups.

Model   Our understanding of a system of interest, or a set of such systems of a certain type – economies, for example – is represented in a theory or a set of theories. For a particular system, it is often convenient to take this a step further and to develop a formal representation of the theory, perhaps one that can be formulated as mathematical equations and programmed into a computer. Such a formal representation is a model of the system of interest. It is obviously not the real system, but as a model of the system it mimics its key properties. If the model is good enough, it can be used to make predictions and is then the basis of the **flight simulator** ideas (q.v.) and can be used in planning.

Monopolistic benefits   A core element of the economic theory of **markets** (q.v.) is that competition will ensure that companies can only achieve 'normal' profits. However, there will be circumstances where, because of location, ownership of scarce resources or the holding of patents, a company might have a monopoly and so can increase profit levels.

Multiple equilibria   Many systems of interest have nonlinear features. There may be positive or negative returns to scale, for example. There are general theorems in mathematics that show that such systems, when expressed as models, have multiple equilibrium solutions. This is a good example of formal mathematics offering insights that can be applied qualitatively.

Neural networks   These are artificial networks that mimic neural functions, albeit in an elementary way. In particular, they can 'learn'.

Networks   Most flows in systems of interest are carried on networks of some kind and the subject of network science has experienced exponential growth.

Nodes   These are the 'points' in the representation of a network. They can be origins or destinations of **flows** (q.v.) or intermediate nodes in a transport or communications network, for example. The most complex biological network is the brain; probably the most complex artificial network is the World Wide Web.

Nonlinear systems   A familiar law of economics is 'the law of diminishing returns' and this illustrates a nonlinear relationship. In this case, the rate of growth is less than the rate of investment, say. It is also possible to have positive returns to scale. Nonlinear systems have particular and important mathematical properties. They can have multiple **equilibrium** (q.v.) solutions; there can be sudden changes at **critical parameter** (q.v.) values – sometimes known as **phase changes** (q.v.); and can change through time – their dynamics is **path dependent** (q.v.)

Operational research   This is the discipline that draws together the techniques for optimizing processes.

Optimization   Many systems are driven by elements that maximize or minimize something. Micro-economics, for example, is underpinned by individuals maximizing **utility functions** (q.v.) or firms maximizing profits. In some circumstances, an organization might want to minimize costs. A transport manager, for example, might want to find the shortest path through a network. Any of these processes can be described generically as optimization processes. There are many elements of mathematics that help the model builder – at an elementary level, for example, the calculus enables us to find the maximization or minimization of functions. More generally, we may want to maximize or minimize a function subject to **constraints** (q.v) and this is the field of **mathematical programming** (q.v.).

Organizational efficiency   This is the usual focus of **performance indicators** (q.v.). Compare also **effective delivery** (q.v.).

Path dependence   This is another example where mathematical formalism accords with intuition: where you can get to depends on where you started! In mathematical terms, this means that the solution of **nonlinear** (q.v.) equations depends on the initial conditions. As a system evolves through time, each step can be thought of as providing a set of initial conditions for the next, and since solutions to the model equations at each step depend on the conditions at the previous step, this is called 'path dependence'.

Pattern recognition   The structure of a crystal is a 'pattern', as is the structure of a city – in the latter case in a great number of dimensions. Much of our theory building is concerned with explaining these patterns and the way they **evolve** (q.v.) and **emerge** (q.v.). There is a field within artificial intelligence that is concerned with pattern recognition. There is a neurophysiological aspect to this: how does the brain recognize patterns? And then how can computers achieve this? This is particularly important in aspects of analysis where there is missing data – a jigsaw puzzle with missing pieces. If the pattern can be recognized, then the missing data can be estimated.

Pedagogy   This is usually about 'how to teach' but we have generalized it to simply 'how to?' or 'how?'. It is then the complement of the **curriculum** (q.v.) generalized to 'what?'.

Performance indicators   It is important to have measures that show how well a system functions – so-called performance indicators. These might relate to **organizational efficiency** (q.v.) – how well a firm, a school or a hospital is performing; or to **effective delivery** (q.v.) to users – customers, consumers or clients. The first of these kinds of performance indicators are commonly used – by city analysts or by governments; the second much less commonly so.

Periodic solutions   These occur when the solutions to a set of equations oscillate. See **Lotka-Volterra** (q.v.) models above as an example.

Phase changes (transitions)   In physics, when ice melts and changes into a liquid – water, this is called a phase change. More broadly, any abrupt change in a **nonlinear system** (q.v.) is also called a phase change.

Planning horizons   It is often convenient to distinguish different planning horizons – for example, short, medium and long, which might be one year, five years and ten years, for example, in a particular situation.

Policy, design and analysis   These represent different kinds of thinking: policy, the specification of objectives and broad **strategy** (q.v.); design, the invention of alternatives; analysis, the investigation of the system of interest and how it works together with a 'What if?' capability to test alternative future developments.

Prey–predator model   This is one of the famous **Lotka-Volterra** (q.v.) models with origins in ecology. It represents the relationship between a predator species whose rate of growth is determined by the prey population. The system usually oscillates: the predator population increases to a point where the prey population starts to diminish, and then the predator population decreases as well – until the cycle begins again.

Production technology   'Technology' is used here in a very broad sense. A 'production technology' is what is needed to make (produce) goods or a service.

Profit maximization   In the simplest economic **models** (q.v.), firms are assumed to maximize profits.

Quality at a price   A difficult challenge in building economic models is the coding of what is well known in practice: that the price of goods or service depends on the quality that is offered. There will be a **market** (q.v.) in quality as well as in price.

Requisite knowledge   This is the 'knowledge' equivalent of **requisite variety** (q.v.): the minimum amount of knowledge that is needed to plan, to run a business or to run a public service, for example.

Requisite variety   Recall that 'variety' (q.v.) is a measure of the complexity of a system. Ashby's Law of Requisite Variety is important in **control theory** (q.v.) but also has a deep and valuable intuitive meaning that can be deployed in a wide range of situations. Consider a system and an associated control system. Ashby's law states that the control system, to be effective, must have at least the variety of the system it is trying to control. The obvious wider applications are in areas such as town planning and zoning, for example.

Scales   Most systems of interest can be viewed in a very aggregate 'upper or coarse' scale way – or at a fine scale, disaggregated. It is useful to be explicit about scale decisions when defining a system of interest and also to recognize that there are relationships between scales.

Shortest path in a network   For many purposes, it is important to be able to find the shortest path through a network, and good computer algorithms have existed to achieve this since the 1950s.

Simplification   Perhaps the most succinct statement of the benefits of seeking to simplify is medieval: Occam's razor. But we also recognize Hoyle's view that the most successful laws tend to be simple but capable of generating **complex** (q.v.) consequences.

Skills   Skills are the mental equipment (and sometimes the associated 'physical' – e.g. for musicians) needed to do a job properly. Is it a kind of knowledge 'beyond theory'?

Slow dynamics   See **fast dynamics** (q.v.).

Spatial interaction models   See **interaction** (q.v.).

Statistical averaging   See **Boltzmann** (q.v.) and **entropy** (q.v.).

Statistical mechanics   See **Boltzmann** (q.v.).

Strategy   An organization, implicitly or explicitly, will have a set of objectives – **policies** (q.v.) for example, to achieve. This could be a business seeking to expand and increase its profits or an army in a battle. An account, or a plan, of how these objectives are to be achieved over time, is a strategy. It is the 'how' something is to be achieved as distinct from the 'what' is to be achieved. It is usually important for any manager or leader to have a strategy, though it is worth bearing in mind the old advice that 'strategy is 5% of the task, implementation is 95%'.

Structuralism   At one level, 'structuralism' can be seen simply as a systems approach to analysis – seeking to understand the underlying structures of a system of interest. However, the more important connotation is that it should make us aware that in seeking to understand a system of interest, to build a theory, we need to dig as deep as possible. In a social system, for example, there may be power relations between actors, which may be hidden from a hypothesis rooted in surface description. Wikipedia cites Alison Assiter (1984) as arguing that it is concerned with 'the real things' that lie beneath the surface or appearance of meaning.

Structure   Systems of interest can be thought of as having a core structure on which functions and activities take place. Human beings, for example, have a skeleton and a set of organs that allow us to function. Cities have the built environment, transport and communications infrastructures, the organizations that make up the economy and so on.

System   This is a key concept. A system is any set of entities and the relationships or interactions between them. To explore any field of knowledge, it is nearly always valuable to define a 'system of interest' and this immediately demonstrates the variety of perspectives that can be adopted: there is no one 'true' way. This encourages prior thought in system definition – and also tolerance in that it is important to recognize that others may have adopted different definitions of a similar system of interest. Forcing different perspectives together can offer important insights. The system concept is also important because it represents a new approach to, an opening up of, a new kind of science, a new kind of knowledge. It contrasts with 'reductionism'.

System representation   Even when a system of interest is well defined, there are usually many alternative ways of representing it – particularly in respect of the level of detail or scale.

System model   See **model** (q.v.).

Technology   Technology is usually taken to refer to 'hardware' – but it should also be taken to encompass 'soft' technology – e.g. the kinds of organizations that can be invented to make maximum use of the internet to find new business propositions – new **production technologies** (q.v.).

Theory   A theory is a set of hypotheses about how some system of interest 'works'. These hypotheses may be more or less well tested and accepted as 'true'. A good theory represents our **understanding** (q.v.) of the system.

Uncertainty principle   An important principle in physics – that at the quantum scale, the observer affects the observation and therefore there is a limit to the accuracy of observation that can be achieved. It is perhaps the only physics concept identified as a superconcept that does not really easily translate into other contexts. It is highlighted because there are sometimes attempts to do this.

Understanding   'Understanding' something is what takes us beyond '**facts**' (q.v.). Our tool kit of relevant concepts and any associated theories or hypotheses achieves this.

Utility function   In economic **models** (q.v.), consumer behaviour is characterized by the maximization of a utility function. This is a way of capturing hypotheses on what drives behaviour.

Variety   The idea of 'variety' is used in cybernetics as a measure of the complexity of a system. This is done through the notion of a state of the system. How many different states of the system are possible? It is intuitively clear that more complex systems have more possible states, and hence 'number of possible states' is defined to be the 'variety' of the system.

VSM model   The viable systems model – see **central nervous system structures** (q.v.) and **Beer's *Brain of the firm* model** (q.v.).

'War room'   The Cabinet Room in England in World War II was in a bunker in Whitehall near the corner of what is now the Foreign Office. It was dominated by a large map table on which the various forces at war were positioned and re-positioned as time moved on. This was presented by Stafford Beer as the only example known to him of an efficient information 'filtering' machine and is held up as a model of what is missing in most organizations – public or private. It can now be visited as a museum.

Wikis and multidimensional classification   The idea of a wiki is best known through Wikipedia. A wiki is essentially computer software that facilitates collaboration. In the case of Wikipedia, this involves the resources of all the authors who are prepared to contribute to entries on the internet. But it also illustrates another idea that emerges from contemporary computers and software: that information can be classified in a multidimensional form – unlike, for example, the forced linear structure of a book.

Notes

1 The knowledge challenge

1 See Andersson *et al.* (1993).
2 Boden (1990).
3 Giddens (1998).
4 '... and doth suffer a sea-change into something rich and strange', Ariel's Song, Act I, Scene ii, *The Tempest*.
5 See Hudson (1972).
6 It is also, more broadly, about the ability to 'think things through' (as Edward Boyle used to say when he was Vice-Chancellor in Leeds). Feynman (1998) put it like this in a lecture in 1963: 'I would like to point out that people are not honest. Scientists are not honest at all, either ... And people usually believe they are ... By honest I don't mean that you only tell what's true. But you make clear the entire situation. You make clear all the information that is required for somebody else who is intelligent to make up their mind.'
7 As argued in Wilson (1996-B).
8 Cisco (2006, p. 3)
9 See Habermas (1974). He distinguished between the technical, the practical and that which empowered individuals.
10 Kline (1987).
11 There is a famous essay by Isaiah Berlin – see Berlin (1978).
12 We will have occasion below to review what different authors currently see as the main driving forces of change in our knowledge base. The argument here is pitched, at least in part, in terms of *systems* and *complexity*. Kaku (1998) discusses three fundamental revolutions: the quantum, computer and biomolecular revolutions. But he also sees a new era of synergies between these. Deutsch (1997), perhaps from a more strictly academic standpoint, saw the driving forces as quantum physics, epistemology, the theory of evolution and the theory of computation. However, there is a substantial overlap between these different pictures, and that is what we will explore in later chapters.
13 Much of the argument will be about science, but the relationship between trends in science and economic and societal trends will be an underlying theme. Ziman (1994) writes (p. 77): '... the relationship of science to society at large has continually grown closer, and more important to both parties. Science, through technology, has become integrated into the workings of our economy, our polity, and our culture, and has developed into one of the major forces for their structural transformation. What we must also realize is that science itself is transformed internally as it reacts to these forces.'
14 Cisco (2008).

15 cf. McKinsey (2007).
16 In particular, the contributions of the arts and the humanities are seriously under-represented.
17 This term was introduced by Tony Becher (1989).
18 See Wilson (1996-A).
19 The 'lateral thinking' idea has been developed in many books by de Bono – for example, de Bono (1977).

2 The knowledge space

1 In seeking to define disciplines, it is sometimes worth bearing in mind what was called the STM approach in Wilson (2000-A): system, theory, methods (and, within the characterization of systems, also breakdowns by scale).
2 See, for example, Jonathan Culler (1981).
3 This background is elaborated from the perspective of this author in Chapter 4 of Wilson (2000-A).
4 Habermas (1974).
5 Bernstein (1976).
6 *Times Literary Supplement*, September 1999.
7 *TLS, op. cit.*
8 This is the universities' version of the agency-structure problem.
9 For example, whether to represent space in models as continuous or discrete.
10 Popper (1959).
11 Dijkstra (1959).
12 I recall from a seminar when I was a student, a philosophy professor, Margery Masterson, I think, arguing that the library classification problem is equivalent to the 'machine translation of languages'.
13 Web 2.0.
14 The 'tribes' argument – cf. Becher (1989).
15 Hoyle (1965).
16 Boltzmann (1896, trans. 1964) showed that a key relationship is $S = k \log W$.
17 $\delta x \delta v > h$.
18 See Arts and Humanities Research Council (2009).
19 Confirmed by Professor Nussbaum in a private communication.
20 This was quoted in an Academia Europaea report of a meeting in Oslo in June 2005.
21 These ideas were introduced to me by Britton Harris – see Harris (1965) – in the 1960s and have stood the test of time in my own tool kit.
22 See Christopher Alexander's (1964) *Notes on the synthesis of form*. Some subjects have unreasonably low status: for example, general diagnosis versus speciality in medicine; or of engineering design.
23 These are based on University of Leeds Schools and Departments.
24 See Cromer (1997).
25 Partnership for 21st Century Skills – see www.21stcenturyskills.org.
26 Hall (1988); it was an American economist (Clopper Almon) who once said to me that putting the word 'urban' before 'economics' had the same effect as putting the word 'horse' before 'doctor'. There are issues of status here!
27 See Gibbons *et al.* (1994) for what those authors call *Mode 2 production*.
28 Wilson (1970).
29 cf. the work of authors like Jaynes (1957, 2003) and the connections to Bayesian statistics.
30 Polya (1945).
31 These are the three key elements in planning. All this emphasizes that invention is

not simply about 'science'. As Feynman (1998) put it: 'We shouldn't think only of technological inventions when we consider progress ... There are an enormous number of the most important nontechnological inventions which mustn't be disregarded. Economic inventions in checks [cheques], for example, and banks, things of this nature. International financial arrangements, and so on, are marvellous inventions.'

32 Wilson (1983 A–D and 1984 A–H).
33 Horgan (1997).
34 We are beginning to find this argument from a number of authors. Kaku (1998), for example – also commenting on Horgan, writes (p. 10), '... the era of reductionism – i.e. reducing everything to its smallest components – is coming to a close'. However, his ongoing science is more specific than that based on the systems argument used here. He argues for the synergy of what he calls the three revolutions – the quantum, the computing and biomiolecular revolutions.
35 Becher (1989): 'When under attack, chemists draw their wagons into a circle and then start firing into the middle.'
36 Bailey (1977): 'Each tribe has a name and a territory, settles its own affairs, goes to war with others, has a distinct language, or at least a distinct dialect, and a variety of ways of demonstrating its apartness from others.'

3 Beyond disciplines: systems and superconcepts

1 See Chapman (1977), Holland (1995, 1998).
2 See Stone (1967, 1970) for examples of both economic and population accounts; and Rees and Wilson (1976) for a more detailed foray into population accounts.
3 Modelling approaches to spatial interaction are summarized in Wilson (2000-A).
4 See Rees and Wilson (1976).
5 Originally articulated as *central place theory* by Christaller (1933).
6 See Wilson (2000-A), Chapter 4.
7 See Wilson (1970).
8 Shannon and Weaver (1949).
9 See Jaynes (2003), for example, and for Fisher information and its wider uses, Frieden (1998).
10 See Ashby (1956).
11 Weaver (1948, 1958).
12 The trajectories of rockets can largely be calculated on this basis!
13 Weaver (1948, 1958).
14 Deutsch (1997), p. 71.
15 See Watson (2001).
16 See, for example, Assiter (1984).
17 Wilson (2000-A) *op. cit.*
18 Rees and Wilson (1976).
19 Leontief (1967), Stone (1967, 1970).
20 Dantzig (1963). He devised the simplex method for linear programming in 1947.
21 These are known as NP-complete problems – see Papadimitriou and Steiglitz (1982) for an account.
22 Technically, these situations can be described as non-linear programming problems. Memories of elementary algebra will trigger the thought that linear equations have unique solutions – but a quadratic equation in a single variable has two. Complex nonlinear systems can have large numbers of possible solutions.
23 Harris and Wilson (1978).
24 Arthur (1988, 1994-A, B).

25 A particular example of a combinatorial problem in modelling urban development arises in what Wilson (1988) called configurational analysis.

26 In the description here, we have implicitly been working with discrete numbers or point patterns, and combinatorics is traditionally associated with this picture. Many of the problems can be stated in terms of continuous (real) numbers or continuous space. The number of possible 'combinations' then becomes infinite, of course. There must be some interesting links to explore between discrete and continuous versions of these problems. There are some classical examples of where continuous mathematics is used to help with discrete problems – for example in the use of Stirling's approximation in statistical mechanics or in the broader applications of entropy in modelling in a variety of disciplines (cf. Wilson, 1970).

27 There is an interesting argument in Deutsch (1997), which essentially says that, because quantum mechanics is fundamentally discrete, and this represents reality, in some sense 'discrete' is more fundamental than 'continuous'!

28 cf. Kelly (1996).

29 In a mathematical programming formulation, for example, constraints are represented by Lagragian multipliers, and specifying these constraints can be an important part of model specification.

30 See Wilson (2000-A).

31 More conventionally, using a notation which has persisted for four decades, from zone i to zone j, $i = 1, \ldots M, j = 1, \ldots N$ in a matrix $\{T_{ij}\}$ – see Wilson (1970).

32 These 'entities' could themselves be systems, and hence the useful notion of 'interacting systems'.

33 Clarke and Wilson (1987-A, B).

34 For an introduction to the shortest path through a network, see Papadimitriou and Steiglitz (1982), Chapters 5 and 6; the algorithm was devised by Dijkstra (1959).

35 Boyce (1984).

36 See Woldenberg (1970).

37 See Wilson (2008).

38 See Wilson (2008).

39 Cohen and Stewart (1994).

40 See Thom (1975); for an introduction to catastrophe theory see Poston and Stewart (1978); see also Wilson (1981).

41 This idea was first drawn to my attention in Barrow (1991) and has recently been emphasized by Deutsch (1997).

42 Holland (1992, 1995, 1998).

43 There is an enormous literature in physics on phase changes but it is now widely recognized that these sudden transitions at critical points are properties of a much wider set of nonlinear systems.

44 Lotka (1925) and Volterra (1938).

45 May (1971).

46 Nowak and May (2000).

47 Harris and Wilson (1978), Wilson (2000-A).

48 Prigogine (1980), Prigogine and Stengers (1984), Gray and Scott (1990).

49 Richardson (1960).

50 Nadler, Gerstein and Shaw (1992), Sadler (1994).

51 Mintzberg (1989).

52 Beer (1994).

53 Oakland (1999).

54 von Bertalanffy (1968).

55 For example, Klir and Valach (1967).
56 See, for example, Beer (1972).
57 See J. Horgan (1997) *The end of science*. Horgan does not consider systems theory and the kind of shift here, except implicitly by reviewing the complexity movement, which he seems to regard as relatively unimportant.
58 Holland (1995), Clarke (ed.) (1996).
59 Wilson (1974) for example.
60 Clarke and Wilson (1987-A, B).
61 Clark (ed.) (1996).
62 Davies and Hersch (1981).
63 Blum (1996).
64 Penrose (1994) makes an interesting distinction – albeit from a theoretical point of view – between top-down algorithms and bottom-up. The former provides a procedure to solve a particular problem; the latter is more loosely organized and 'gradually improves, eventually giving a good solution to the problem in hand'. This relates to neural network methods (cf. section 3.7.4) and, more generally, to what Hillis (1985, 1995, 1998) calls 'connection machines'.
65 Thomsen (1997).
66 Kelly (1996).
67 Holland (1995, 1998).
68 Wikis provide the software for collaboration most famously exhibited by Wikipedia.
69 Aleksander and Morton (1990); Golden (1996).
70 See Wilson (2000-A), Chapter 8.
71 See the Hopfield argument, cited in Kaku (1998).
72 von Neumann (1966).
73 In a particular context, see Birkin, Clarke, Clarke and Wilson (1996).
74 Davenport and Prusak (1998).

4 Knowledge development

1 This author thought he had invented the concept of 'enabling disciplines', but it turns up in Ziman (1994), p. 33, though in a slightly different form – e.g. with microelectronics as an enabling technology in industry.
2 See Singh (1997).
3 Thom (1972).
4 Bear in mind Moore's law: that computing power doubles every 18 months. Kaku (1998) says that this 'was first stated in 1965 by Gordon Moore, co-founder of the Intel Corporation'. However, it is now thought that the physical limit of miniaturization is almost reached.
5 For example, see the programme of the Institute of Informatics in Leeds.
6 A good account is provided by Kaku (1994).
7 See Kaku and Thompson (1987, 2nd edn, 1995).
8 See Kaku (1998), Chapter 4, for an excellent discussion of the possibilities.
9 See almost any advanced book on statistical mechanics.
10 Beck and Schlogl (1993).
11 NERC is the Natural Environment Research Council.
12 See Michael Porter (1990).
13 Wilson (1970).
14 As described by Watson (1968) himself, for example, in *The double helix*.
15 Francis Crick (1981).
16 Kaku (1998) p. 41.

17 Goodwin (1994).
18 Lotka (1925), Volterra (1938).
19 May (1971, 1973).
20 Kaku (1998) provides an excellent summary of the impact of what he calls the 'biomolecular revolution' on medicine.
21 Sir Eric Ash, when he was rector of Imperial College, used to say that if he wanted to show some visitors some good science, he took them to an engineering department! And vice versa.
22 Alexander (1964).
23 Harris (1965).
24 Anderson, Arrow and Pines (1988); Arthur (1988, 1994-A, 1994-B).
25 Krugman (1996).
26 Rosser (1991).
27 See, for example, Nelson and Winter (1982).
28 Foster and Beesley (1963).
29 This is a process known as 'disintermediation' or, in other words, 'cutting out the middleman'!
30 cf. The concept of 'abstract modes' introduced by Quandt and Baumol (1966).
31 Orcutt (1957).
32 Gilbert (1995).
33 See Wilson (2006) for a recent attempt.
34 Habermas (1974).
35 This was Bentham's 'greatest happiness for the greatest possible number'.
36 Kant's categorical imperative essentially says that you shouldn't do to others what you would not want them to do to you. It handles questions of crime well but is less conclusive on some of the more difficult questions of politics.
37 Leontief (1967).
38 Clarke and Wilson (1987-A, 1987-B).
39 See Mintzberg (1989).
40 Glass (1996).
41 Hawkins and Gell-Mann (1992).
42 Lakoff and Johnson (1980).
43 Wilson (1983-A).
44 Christopher Frayling's phrase; 1999 TV series on Royal College of Art, BBC2.
45 Jude Kelly, Convocation Lecture, University of Leeds, 23 June 2001.
46 See Kaku (1998), Chapter 4.

5 Requisite knowledge

1 Ashby's (1956) law of requisite variety; this idea is picked up by and developed in relation to organizations by Morgan (1997).
2 For example, if standards are critical, as in medicine, then the technostructure is important.
3 And here, we are using innovation in a broad sense. Ackoff (1999) emphasizes (p. 163) that much progress comes from the creative re-arrangement of what we already know.
4 See Christensen (1997).
5 Christensen in his own summary expands on the argument.
6 cf. Stafford Beer's (1972) *Brain of the firm* argument; see also Chapter 4 in Morgan (1997).
7 The clearest example here is the introduction of a new transport mode – cf. Quandt and Baumol (1966).

8 We might also add that what all organizations are trying to achieve is a *growth strategy*, and that we might think of this as a superconcept.
9 cf. Geoffrey Moore's notions of 'core and context'.
10 Colloquially, short run, middle run and long run?
11 cf. the BCG (Boston Consulting Group) matrix.
12 Oakland (1999).
13 See Goold and Campbell (1987).
14 Russell Ackoff – as summarized in Ackoff (1999) – remains very readable and full of ideas. He also connects very strongly to the theme of this book through his *systems* focus.
15 See Hodgson and White (2001).
16 Hodgson and White (2001), p. 203, quote Machiavelli as saying 500 years ago: 'There is nothing more difficult to take in hand, more perilous to conduct, or more uncertain in its success, than to take the lead in the introduction of a new order of things.'
17 See Garvin (2000) for a good example.
18 Andersson *et al.* (1993), first referred to in Chapter 1.
19 Mintzberg (1989).
20 Christensen (1997).

6 Knowledge power and universities

1 These three activities constitute the third arm (or 'leg' or 'mission') to complement teaching and research.
2 Gates (1999).
3 There are also some specific issues, for example, concerned with the production of students with a decent maths background.
4 JISC, the Joint Information Systems Committee, funded by HEFCE, handle much of this.
5 REF – the Research Excellence Framework which will replace the RAE some time after 2009.
6 The two elements combined – the new map of knowledge and the explosion of the volume of knowledge – generate a combinatorial problem: myriads of different 'packages'.
7 Ziman (1994) p. 2 and p. 232 respectively.
8 Nor are the costs of electronic delivery well understood.
9 As we will see below, there is now considerable debate about deregulation and 'freeing' universities to charge market prices for courses.
10 The College of Law and BPP Ltd now have degree awarding powers under recent legislation.
11 Since 1997, the teaching unit of resource has been more or less maintained.
12 There have been many initiatives that seek to address this. The latest Government programme is described in National Science Learning Centre (2008) *The STEM framework*, York.
13 Wilson (2000-B).
14 The contributions to major public policy areas of health, education and crime, for example, have not been on a 'big science' scale.
15 There is a classic organization design problem here: however you divide up the organization, there will be a need to cross 'boundaries'.
16 Indeed, it can be argued that universities have sustained extraordinary growth rates over the last decade and a half. What universities have managed to do, in general, is to professionalize their management while at the same time remaining accountable to large bodies of staff – no mean feat!

17 In Leeds, for example, there are over 60.
18 Overheads are a university problem, because outside organizations often perceive universities to be 'cheap' and that they ought to remain cheap; cf. the American situation with the Government 'audit' and agreed recovery rates.
19 Strategic business units.

7 Employers in the knowledge economy

1 cf. the corporate universities' movement.
2 Birkin *et al.* (1996).
3 cf. the classic Hotelling (1929) problem: ice cream men on a linear beach.
4 For example, if standards are critical, as in medicine, then the technostructure is important.
5 In extreme cases, this will be the core of the business – with franchise operations, for instance.
6 For example, the biotech industry.
7 See, for example, Mantegna and Stanley (2000).
8 For example, if standards are critical, as in medicine, then the technostructure is important.
9 Birkin *et al.* (1996).
10 Clarke and Wilson (1987-A, B).
11 For example, with PFI capital schemes.

8 Knowledge power: a sea change?

1 SCORE, the science community representing education, a partnership of learned societies.
2 ACME, Advisory Committee on Mathematics Education, representing the mathematics community.

Appendix 3 Glossary of superconcepts

1 '!' denotes 'factorial', for example, $4! = 4 \times 3 \times 2 \times 1$. $N! = N \times (n-1) \times (N-2) \times \ldots \times 4 \times 3 \times 2 \times 1$.
2 Herbert Simon (e.g. 1983, 1996) introduced the 'satisficing' concept.
3 Wilson (1970).

Bibliography

Ackoff, R. L. (1999) *Ackoff's best: his classic writings on management*, John Wiley, New York.

Agre, P. E. (1996) *The dynamic structure of everyday life*, Cambridge University Press, Cambridge.

Aleksander, I. and Morton, H. (1990) *An introduction to neural computing*, Chapman and Hall, London.

Alexander, C. (1964) *Notes on the synthesis of form*, Harvard University Press, Cambridge, MA.

Amin, A. and Roberts, J. (2008) *Community, economic activity and organization*, Oxford University Press, Oxford.

Amin, A. and Thrift, N. (2002) *Cities: reimagining the urban*, Polity Press, Cambridge.

Anderson, P. W., Arrow, K. J., and Pines, D. (eds) (1988) *The economy as an evolving complex system*, Addison Wesley, Menlo Park, CA.

Andersson, A. E., Batten, D. F., Kobayashi, K. and Yoshikawa, K. (eds) (1993) *The cosmo-creative society: logistical networks in a dynamic economy*, Springer-Verlag, Berlin.

Andersson, C. (2005) *Urban evolution*, Department of Physical Resource Theory, Chalmers University of Technology, Goteborg.

Angier, N. (2007) *The canon: the beautiful basics of science*, Faber & Faber, London.

Arthur, W. B. (1988) 'Urban systems and historical path dependence', in J. H. Ausubel and R. Herman (eds) *Cities and their vital systems: infrastructure, past, present and future*, National Academy Press, Washington, DC.

Arthur, W. B. (1994-A) *Increasing returns and path dependence in the economy*, University of Michigan Press, Ann Arbor, MI.

Arthur, W. B. (1994-B) 'Inductive reasoning and bounded rationality', *American Economic Association Papers and Proceedings*, 84, pp. 406–11.

Arts and Humanities Research Council (2009) *Leading the world: the economic impact of UK arts and humanities research*, AHRC, Bristol.

Ashby, W. R. (1956) *An introduction to cybernetics*, Chapman and Hall, London.

Assiter, A. (1984) Althusser and structuralism, *British Journal of Sociology*, 35, pp. 272–96.

Atkins, P. (2003) *Galileo's finger: the ten great ideas of science*, Oxford University Press, Oxford.

Baghai, M., Coley, S. and White, D. (1999) *The alchemy of growth*, Perseus Publications, Cambridge, MA.

Bailey, F. G. (1977) *Morality and expediency: the folklore of academic politics*, Blackwell, Oxford.

Bak, P. (1997) *How nature works: the science of self-organized criticality*, Oxford University Press, Oxford.

Baldi, P. and Brunak, S. A. (1998) *Bioinformatics: the machine learning approach*, MIT Press, Cambridge, MA.

Ball, P. (2009) *Nature's patterns – 1: shapes*, Oxford University Press, Oxford.

Barabasi, A-L. (2002) *Linked: the new science of networks*, Perseus Publishing, Cambridge, MA.

Barrow, J. (1991) *Theories of everything*, Oxford University Press, Oxford.

Becher, T. (1989) *Academic tribes and territories*, Open University Press, Milton Keynes.

Beck, C. and Schlogl, F. (1993) *Thermodynamics of chaotic systems*, Cambridge University Press, Cambridge.

Beck, U. (1992) *The risk society*, Sage Publications, London.

Becker, G. S. (1965) 'A theory of the allocation of time', *Economic Journal*, 75, pp. 488–517.

Beer, S. (1972, 2nd edn, 1981) *Brain of the firm*, John Wiley, Chichester.

Beer, S. (1994) *Designing freedom*, John Wiley, Chichester.

Behe, M. J. (1996) *Darwin's black box: the biochemical challenge to evolution*, The Free Press, New York.

Berlin, I. (1978) 'The hedgehog and the fox', in H. Hardy and R. Hausher (eds) *Isaiah Berlin: the proper study of mankind*, Chatto and Windus, London.

Bernstein, R. (1976) *The restructuring of social and political theory*, Blackwell, Oxford.

Bertalanffy, L. von (1968) *General system theory*, Braziller, New York.

Bertuglia, C. S. and Vaio, F. (2005) *Nonlinearity, chaos and complexity: the dynamics of natural and social systems*, Oxford University Press, Oxford.

Birkin, M., Clarke, G. P., Clarke, M. and Wilson, A. G. (1996) *Intelligent GIS: location decisions and strategic planning*, Geoinformation International, Cambridge.

Blum, B. I. (1996) *Beyond programming: to a new era of design*, Oxford University Press, New York.

Bochel, H. and Duncan, S. (eds) (2007) *Making policy in theory and practice*, The Policy Press, Bristol.

Boden, M. A. (1990) *The creative mind: myths and mechanisms*, Weidenfeld and Nicholson, London.

Bok, D. (1986) *Higher learning*, Harvard University Press, Cambridge, MA.

Bok, D. (2001) *The trouble with government*, Harvard University Press, Cambridge, MA.

Boltzmann, L. (1896, trans. S. G. Brush, 1964) *Lectures on gas theory*, University of California Press, Berkeley and Los Angeles.

Bono, E. de (1977) *Lateral thinking*, Penguin, Harmondsworth.

Boyce, D. E. (1984) 'Urban transportation network-equilibrium and design models: recent achievements and future prospects', *Environment and Planning*, A, 16, pp. 1445–74.

Brockman, J. (ed.) (1995) *The third culture: beyond the scientific revolution*, Simon & Schuster, New York.

Buzan, T. with Buzan, B. (1993) *The mind map book*, BBC Publications, London.

Caldarelli, G. (2007) *Scale-free networks: complex webs in nature and technology*, Oxford University Press, Oxford.

Callender, C. and Huggett, N. (2001) *Physics meets philosophy at the Planck scale*, Cambridge University Press, Cambridge.

Camazine, S., Deneubourg, J-L., Franks, N. R., Sneyd, J., Theraulaz, G. and Bonabeau, E. (2001) *Self-organisation in biological systems*, Princeton University Press, Princeton and Oxford.

Carroll, M. L. (1996) *Cyberstrategies: how to build an internet-based information system*, Van Nostrand Reinhold, New York.

Carroll, S. B. (2008) *The making of the fittest: DNA and the ultimate forensic record of evolution*, Quercus, London.

Chaitin, G. (2005) *Meta math! The quest for omega*, Pantheon, New York.

Chapman, G. T. (1977) *Human and environmental systems*, Academic Press, London.

Checkland, P. (1981) *Systems thinking, systems practice*, John Wiley, Chichester.

Checkland, P. and Scholes, J. (1991) *Soft systems methodology in action*, John Wiley, Chichester.

Checkland, P. and Holwell, S. (1998) *Information, systems and information systems*, John Wiley, Chichester.

Christaller, W. (1933) *Die centralen Orte in Suddeutschland*, Gustav Fisher, Jena; English translation by C. W. Baskin (1996) *Central places in Southern Germany*, Prentice Hall, Englewood Cliffs, NJ.

Christensen, C. M. (1997) *The innovator's dilemma*, Harper Business, New York.

Cisco (2006) *Technology in schools*, Cisco Systems Inc., San Jose, CA.

Cisco (2008) *Equipping every learner for the 21st Century*, Cisco Systems Inc, San Jose, CA.

Clarke, B. R. (1998) *Creating entrepreneurial universities: organizational pathways of transformation*, Pergamon, Oxford.

Clarke, B. R. (2004) *Sustaining change in universities: continuities in case studies and concepts*, Open University Press, Maidenhead.

Clarke, G. P. (ed.) (1996) *Microsimulation for urban and regional policy analysis*, Pion, London.

Clarke, G. P. and Wilson, A. G. (1987-A) 'Performance indicators and model-based planning I: the indicator movement and the possibilities for urban planning', *Sistemi Urbani*, 2, pp. 79–123.

Clarke, G. P. and Wilson, A. G. (1987-B) 'Performance indicators and model-based planning II: model-based approaches', *Sistemi Urbani*, 9, pp. 138–65.

Cohen, J. and Stewart, I. (1994) *The collapse of chaos: discovering simplicity in a complex world*, Viking, London.

Cornford, F. M. (1908) *Microcosmographia academica: being a guide for the young academic politician*, Bowes and Bowes, Cambridge.

Coveney, P. and Highfield, R. (1995) *Frontiers of complexity: the search for order in a chaotic world*, Faber & Faber, London.

Crick, F. (1981) *Life itself*, Simon & Schuster, New York.

Cromer, A. (1997) *Connected knowledge: science, philosophy and education*, Oxford University Press, Oxford.

Culler, J. (1981) *The pursuit of signs: semiotics, literature and deconstruction*, Routledge and Kegan Paul, London.

Dantzig, G. B. (1963) *Linear programming and extensions*, Princeton University Press, Princeton.

Davenport, T. H. and Prusak, L. (1998) *Working knowledge: how organizations manage what they know*, Harvard Business School Press, Boston.

Davies, L. (ed.) (1991) *Handbook of genetic algorithms*, Van Nostrand Reinhold, New York.

Davies, P. J. and Hersch, R. (1981) *The mathematical experience*, Birkhauser, Boston.

Davis, S. and Meyer, C. (1998) *Blur: the speed of change in the connected economy*, Capstone, Oxford.

Desai, R. C. and Kapral, R. (2009) *Dynamics of self-organised and self-assembled structures*, Cambridge University Press, Cambridge.

Deutsch, D. (1997) *The fabric of reality*, Allen Lane, The Penguin Press, Harmondsworth.

Devlin, K. (2004) *The millennium problems: the seven greatest unsolved mathematical puzzles of our time*, Granta Publications, London.

Dijkstra, E. W. (1959) 'A note on two problems in connection with graphs', *Numerische Mathematik*, 1, pp. 269–71.

Dopfer, K. (2005) *The evolutionary foundations of economics*, Cambridge University Press, Cambridge.

Dorogovtsev, S. N. and Mendes, J. F. F. (2003) *Evolution of networks: from biological nets to the internet and WWW*, Oxford University Press, Oxford.

Drucker, P. F. (1989) *The new realities*, Heinemann, London.

Epstein, J. M. and Axtell, R. (1996) *Growing artificial societies: social science from the bottom up*, MIT Press, Cambridge, MA.

Feynman, R. P., Leighton, R. B. and Sands, M. (1963) *The Feynman lectures on physics*, Addison-Wesley, Reading, MA.

Feynman, R. P. (1998) *The meaning of it all*, Allen Lane, The Penguin Press, Harmondsworth.

Forrester, J. W. (1969) *Urban dynamics*, MIT Press, Cambridge, MA.

Foster, C. D. (2005) *British government in crisis: the third English revolution*, Hart Publishing, Oxford and Portland, OR.

Foster, C. D. and Beesley, M. E. (1963) 'Estimating the social benefit of constructing an underground railway in London', *Journal of the Royal Statistical Society*, A, 126, pp. 46–92.

Frieden, B. R. (1998) *Physics from Fisher information: a unification*, Cambridge University Press, Cambridge.

Gabriel, R. P. (1996) *Patterns of software: tales from the software community*, Oxford University Press, Oxford.

Garvin, D. A. (2000) *Learning in action*, Harvard Business School Press, Boston.

Gates, W. (1999) *Business @ the speed of light*, Penguin, London.

Gibbons, M., Limoges, C., Nowotny, H., Schwartzman, S., Scott, P. and Trow, M. (1994) *The new production of knowledge: the dynamics of science and research in contemporary societies*, Sage Publications, London.

Giddens, A. (1998) *The third way: renewal of social democracy*, Polity Press, Cambridge.

Gilbert, G. N. (1995) 'Using computer simulation to study social phenomena', *Bulletin de Methodologie Sociologique*, 47, pp. 99–111.

Gladwell, M. (2008) *Outliers: the story of success*, Allen Lane, The Penguin Press, Harmondsworth.

Glass, N. M. (1996) *Management masterclass: a practical guide to the new realities of business*, Nicholas Brealey, London.

Golden, R. M. (1996) *Mathematical methods for neural network analysis and design*, MIT Press, Cambridge, MA.

Goodwin, B. (1994) *How the leopard changed its spots*, Weidenfeld and Nicholson, London.

Goold, M. and Campbell, A. (1987) *Strategies and styles: the role of the centre in managing diversified corporations*, Blackwell, Oxford.

Graham, S. and Marvin, S. (1996) *Telecommunications and the city*, Routledge, London.

Gray, P. and Scott, S. (1990) *Chemical oscillations and instabilities*, Oxford University Press, Oxford. [via Coveney and Highfield]

Habermas, J. (1974) *Theory and practice*, Heinemann, London.

Hall, P. (1988) *Cities of tomorrow*, Blackwell, Oxford.

Harris, B. (1965) 'Urban development models: new tools for planners', *Journal of the American Institute of Planners*, 31, pp. 90–5.

Harris, B. and Wilson, A. G. (1978) 'Equilibrium values and dynamics of attractiveness terms in production-constrained spatial-interaction models', *Environment and Planning*, A, 10, pp. 371–88.

Hassell, M. P. (2000) *The spatial and temporal dynamics of host-parasite interactions*, Oxford University Press, Oxford.

Hawken, P. (1993) *The ecology of commerce*, Harper-Collins, New York.

Hawkins, J. A. and Gell-Mann, M. (eds) (1992) *The evolution of human languages*, Addison-Wesley, Reading, MA.

Hillis, W. D. (1985) *The connection machine*, MIT Press, Cambridge, MA.

Hillis, W. D. (1995) *The pattern on the stone*, Weidenfeld and Nicholson, London.

Hillis, W. D. (1998) 'Close to the singularity', in J. Brockman (ed.) (1995) *op.cit.*, pp. 378–88.

Hodgson, P. and White, R. P. (2001) *Relax, it's only uncertainty*, Prentice Hall, Harlow.

Holland, J. H. (1992) *Adaptation in natural and artificial systems: an introductory analysis with applications in biology, control and artificial intelligence*, MIT Press, Cambridge, MA.

Holland, J. H. (1995) *Hidden order: how adaptation builds complexity*, Addison-Wesley, Reading, MA.

Holland, J. H. (1998) *Emergence*, Addison-Wesley, Reading, MA.

Horgan, J. (1997) *The end of science*, Little Brown and Co. (UK), London.

Hotelling, H. (1929) 'Stability in competition', *Economic Journal*, 39, pp. 41–57.

Hoyle, F. (1965) *Of men and galaxies*, Heinemann, London.

Hudson, L. (1972) *The cult of the fact*, Jonathan Cape, London.

Jacobs, J. (1970) *The economy of cities*, Jonathan Cape, London.

Jaynes, E. T. (1957) 'Information theory and statistical mechanics', *Physical Review*, 106, pp. 620–30.

Jaynes, E. T. (2003) *Probability theory*, Cambridge University Press, Cambridge.

Johnson, G. (1994) *University politics: F. M. Cornford's Cambridge and his advice to the young academic politician*, Cambridge University Press, Cambridge.

Jordan, M. I. (ed.) (1999) *Learning in graphical models*, MIT Press, Cambridge, MA.

Kaku, M. (1994) *Hyperspace: a scientific odyssey through the tenth dimension*, Oxford University Press, Oxford.

Kaku, M. (1998) *Visions: how science will revolutionise the twenty-first century and beyond*, Oxford University Press, Oxford.

Kaku, M. and Thompson, J. (1987, 2nd edn, 1995) *Beyond Einstein: the cosmic quest for the theory of the universe*, Oxford University Press, Oxford.

Kelly, S. (1996) *Data warehousing*, John Wiley, Chichester.

Kline, S. J. (1987) 'The logical necessity of multidisciplinarity: a consistent view of the world', *Bulletin of Science, Technology and Society*, 6, pp. 1–26. [via Favre *et al*]

Klir, J. and Valach, M. (1967) *Cybernetic modelling*, Iliffe, London.

Kronman, A. T. (2007) *Education's end: why our colleges and universities have given up on the meaning of life*, Yale University Press, New Haven, CT.

Krugman, P. R. (1996) *The self-organizing economy*, Blackwell, Oxford.

Lakoff, G. and Johnson, M. (1980) *Metaphors we live by*, The University of Chicago Press, Chicago.

Leadbeater, C. (2000) *The weightless society: living in the new economy bubble*, Texere, New York.

Leontief, W. (1967) *Input–output analysis*, Oxford University Press, Oxford.

Lesourne, J., Orlean, A. and Walliser, B. (2006) *Evolutionary micro-economics*, Springer, Berlin.

Lotka, A. J. (1925) *The elements of physical biology*, Williams and Wilkins, Baltimore.

McCann, P. (2001) *Urban and regional economics*, Oxford University Press, Oxford.

McKinsey and Company (2007) *How the world's best school systems come out on top*, McKinsey and Company, London.

Maddox, J. (1998) *What remains to be discovered: mapping the secrets of the universe, the origins of life and the future of the human race*, Macmillan, Basingstoke and Oxford.

Mantegna, R. N. and Stanley, H. E. (2000) *An introduction to econophysics: correlations and complexity in finance*, Cambridge University Press, Cambridge.

May, R. M. (1971) Stability in multi-species community models, *Mathematical Biosciences*, 12, pp. 59–79.

May, R. M. (1973) *Stability and complexity in model ecosystems*, Princeton University Press, Princeton.

Meadows, D. H. (2009) *Thinking in systems: a primer*, Earthscan, London.

Mintzberg, H. (1989) *Structure in fives: designing effective organisations*, Prentice-Hall, Englewood Cliffs, NJ.

Mintzberg, H. and Quinn, J. B. (1992) *The strategy process*, Prentice-Hall, Englewood Cliff, NJ.

Moore, G. A. (2005) *Dealing with Darwin*, Penguin, New York.

Morgan, G. (1997) *Images of organisation*, Sage Publications, London.

Mullan, J. (2006) *How novels work*, Oxford University Press, Oxford.

Nadler, D. A., Gerstein, M. S., Shaw, R. B. and associates (1992) *Organisational architecture: designs for changing organisations*, Jossey-Bass, San Francisco.

National Academy of Sciences, National Academy of Engineering and Institute of Medicine (2007) *Rising above the gathering storm: energizing and employing America for a brighter economic future*, The National Academies Press, Washington, DC.

National Science Learning Centre (2008) *The STEM framework*, University of York, York.

Neilsen, M. A. and Chuang, I. L. (2000) *Quantum computation and quantum information*, Cambridge University Press, Cambridge.

Nelson, R. R. and Winter, S. G. (1982) *An evolutionary theory of economic change*, Belknap Press of Harvard University Press, Cambridge, MA.

Neumann, J. von (1966) *Theory of self-reproducing automata*, University of Illinois Press, Urbana.

Newman, M., Barabasi, A-L. and Watts, D. J. (2006) *The structure and dynamics of networks*, Princeton University Press, Princeton.

Nicolis, G. and Prigogine, I. (1977) *Self-organisation in non-equilibrium systems: from dissipative structures to order through fluctuations*, John Wiley, Chichester.

Nicolis, G. and Prigogine, I. (1989) *Exploring complexity*, W. H. Freeman, New York.

Nowak, M. A. (2006) *Evolutionary dynamics: exploring the equations of life*, Belknap Press of Harvard University Press, Cambridge, MA.

Nowak, M. A. and May, R. M. (2000) *Virus dynamics: mathematical principles of immunology and virology*, Oxford University Press, Oxford.

Nutley, S. M., Walter, I. and Davies, H. T. O (2007) *Using evidence: how research can inform public services*, The Policy Press, Bristol.

Oakland, J. (1999) *Total organisational excellence*, Butterworth-Heinemann, Oxford.

Orcutt, G. H. (1957) 'A new type of socio-economic system', *Review of Economic Statistics*, 58, pp. 773–97.

Palsson, B. O. (2006) *Systems biology: properties of reconstructed networks*, Cambridge University Press, Cambridge.

Papadimitriou and Steiglitz (1982) *Combinatorial optimization: algorithms and complexity*, Prentice Hall, Englewood Cliffs, NJ; Dover edition, 1998.

Pastor-Satorras, R. and Vespignani, A. (2004) *Evolution and structure of the internet: a statistical physics approach*, Cambridge University Press, Cambridge.

Penrose, R. (1989) *The emperor's new mind: concerning computers, minds, and the laws of physics*, Oxford University Press, Oxford.

Penrose, R. (1994) *Shadows of the mind: a search for the missing science of consciousness*, Oxford University Press, Oxford.

Penrose, R. (1995) 'Consciousness involves noncomputable ingredients', in J. Brockman (ed.) (1995) *op. cit.*, pp. 239–57.

Penrose, R. (2004) *The road to reality: a complete guide to the laws of the universe*, Jonathan Cape, London.

Polya, G. (1945) *How to solve it: a new aspect of mathematical method*, Princeton University Press, Princeton.

Popper, K. (1959) *The logic of scientific discovery*, Hutchinson, London.

Porter, M. (1990) *The competitive advantage of nations*, The Free Press, New York.

Poston, T. and Stewart, I. (1978) *Catastrophe theory and its applications*, Pitman, London.

Prigogine, I. (1980) *From being to becoming: time and complexity in physical science*, Freeman, San Francisco.

Prigogine, I. and Stengers, I. (1984) *Order out of chaos: man's new dialogue with nature*, Heinemann, London.

Primack, J. and Abrams, N. E. (2006) *The view from the centre of the universe: discovering our extraordinary place in the cosmos*, Fourth Estate, London.

Quandt, R. E. and Baumol, W. J. (1966) 'The demand for abstract transport modes: theory and measurement', *Journal of Regional Science*, 6, pp. 13–26.

Rees, M. (1999) *Just six numbers: the deep forces that shape the universe*, Weidenfeld and Nicholson, London.

Rees, P. H. and Wilson, A. G. (1976) *Spatial population analysis*, Edward Arnold, London.

Richardson, L. F. (1960) *Arms and insecurity*, The Boxwood Press, Pittsburgh.

Robinson, K. (2009) *The element: how finding your passion changes everything*, Allen Lane, The Penguin Press, London.

Roos, J., Roos, G., Edvinsson, L. and Dragonetti, N. C. (1997) *Intellectual capital: navigating in the new business landscape*, Macmillan, Basingstoke.

Rosser, J. B. Jr. (1991) *From catastrophe to chaos: a general theory of economic discontinuities*, Kluwer Academic Publishers, Boston.

Ruelle, D. (2002) *The thermodynamic formalism: the mathematical structure of equilibrium statistical mechanics*, Cambridge University Press, Cambridge.

Sadler, P. (1991) *Designing organisations*, Mercury Books, London.

Schlecty, P. C. (2005) *Creating great schools: six critical systems at the heart of educational innovation*, Jossey-Bass, San Francisco.

Sennett, R. (1998) *The corrosion of character*, W. W. Norton, New York.

Sennett, R. (2006) *The culture of the new capitalism*, Yale University Press, New Haven, CT.

Sennett, R. (2008) *The craftsman*, Allen Lane, The Penguin Press, London.

Shannon, C. and Weaver, W. (1949) *The mathematical theory of communication*, University of Illinois Press, Urbana.

Simon, H. A. (1983) *Reason in human affairs*, Stanford University Press, Stanford.

Simon, H. A. (1996, 3rd edn) *The sciences of the artificial*, MIT Press, Cambridge, MA.

Singh, S. (1997) *Fermat's last theorem*, Fourth Estate, London.

Stern, N. (2007) *The economics of climate change*, Cambridge University Press, Cambridge.

Stone, R. (1967) *Mathematics in the social sciences*, Chapman and Hall, London.

Stone, R. (1970) *Mathematical models of the economy*, Chapman and Hall, London.

Tapscott, D. and Williams, A. D. (2006) *Wikinomics: how mass collaboration changes everything*, Atlantic Books, London.

Thom, R. (1972) *Structural stability and morphogenesis*, W. A. Benjamin, Reading, MA.

Thomsen, E. (1997) *OLAP solutions: building multidimensional information systems*, John Wiley, New York.

Tushman, M. L. and O'Reilly III, C. A. (1998) *Winning through innovation*, Harvard Business School Press, Boston.

Urry, J. (2003) *Global complexity*, Polity Press, Cambridge.

Volterra, V. (1938) 'Population growth, equilibria and extinction under specified breeding conditions: a development and extension of the theory of the logistic curve', *Human Biology*, 10.

Wagner, C. S. (2008) *The new invisible college: science for development*, Brookings Institution Press, Washington, DC.

Watson, P. (2001) *A terrible beauty: a history of the people and ideas that shaped the modern mind*, Weidenfeld and Nicholson, London.

Watson, J. D. (1968) *The double helix*, Atheneum, New York.

Watts, D. J. (1999) *Small worlds: the dynamics of networks between order and randomness*, Princeton University Press, Princeton.

Weaver, W. (1948) 'Science and complexity', *American Scientist*, 36, pp. 536–44.

Weaver, W. (1958) *A quarter century in the natural sciences*, Annual Report, The Rockefeller Foundation, New York, pp. 7–122.

Weiner, N. (1994 edn) *Invention*, MIT Press, Cambridge, MA.

Whalley, L. (2001) *The ageing brain*, Weidenfeld and Nicholson, London.

Wilkinson, R. (2005) *The impact of inequality: how to make sick societies healthier*, New Press, New York and London.

Wilson, A. G. (1970) *Entropy in urban and regional modelling*, Pion, London.

Wilson, A. G. (1974) *Urban and regional models in geography and planning*, John Wiley, Chichester and New York

Wilson, A. G. (1981) *Catastrophe theory and bifurcation: applications to urban and regional systems*, Croom Helm, London; University of California Press, Berkeley.

Wilson, A. G. (1983-A) *Varieties of structuralism*, Working Paper 350, School of Geography, University of Leeds.

Wilson, A. G. (1983-B) 'From the specific to the general', *Times Higher Education Supplement*, 14 October.

Wilson, A. G. (1983-C) 'Billiard cue', *Times Higher Education Supplement*, 18 November.

Wilson, A. G. (1983-D) 'The best of both worlds?', *Times Higher Education Supplement*, 23 December.

Wilson, A. G. (1984-A) 'New foundations laid for a general approach', *Times Higher Education Supplement*, 10 February.

Wilson, A. G. (1984-B) 'Adding a degree of subtlety', *Times Higher Education Supplement*, 23 March.

Wilson, A. G. (1984-C) 'Understanding each other', *Times Higher Education Supplement*, 20 April.

Wilson, A. G. (1984-D) 'Catastrophe theory', *Times Higher Education Supplement*, 25 May.

Wilson, A. G. (1984-E) 'When decoding is encoding', *Times Higher Education Supplement*, 29 June.

Wilson, A. G. (1984-F) 'Reticular research', *Times Higher Education Supplement*, 20 July.

Wilson, A. G. (1984-G) 'Jam on the bread and butter', *Times Higher Education Supplement*, 28 September.

Wilson, A. G. (1984-H) 'Solving the problems', *Times Higher Education Supplement*, 30 November.

Wilson, A. G. (1985-A) *Useful philosophy*, Working Paper 437, School of Geography, University of Leeds.

Wilson, A. G. (1985-B) 'Humble role on the world's stage', *Times Higher Education Supplement*, 18 March.

Wilson, A. G. (1988) 'Configurational analysis and urban and regional theory', *Sistemi Urbani*, 10, pp. 51–62.

Wilson, A. G. (1991) 'Choices in higher education: the academic agenda', in *The future of higher education*, Chaplaincy, University of Leeds, November.

Wilson, A. G. (1992) 'New maps of old terrain', *Times Higher Education Supplement*, 1 May.

Wilson, A. G. (1996-A) 'Conceptual capability', *Capability*, 2, 80.

Wilson, A. G. (1996-B) *Employability and graduateness*, Presentation to a conference of Science Deans, University of Leeds, November.

Wilson, A. G. (2000-A) *Complex spatial systems: the modelling foundations of urban and regional analysis*, Prentice Hall, Harlow.

Wilson, A. G. (2000-B) 'The widening access debate: student flows to universities and associated performance indicators', *Environment and Planning*, A, 32, pp. 2019–31.

Wilson, A. G. (2006) 'Ecological and urban systems models: some explorations of similarities in the context of complexity theory', *Environment and Planning*, A, 38, pp. 633–46.

Wilson, A. G. (2007) 'A general representation for urban and regional models', *Computers, Environment and Urban Systems*, 31, pp. 148–61.

Wilson, A. G. (2008) 'Boltzmann, Lotka and Volterra and spatial structural evolution: an integrated methodology for some dynamical systems', *Journal of the Royal Society, Interface*, 5, pp. 865–71, *doi:10.1098/rsif.2007.1288.*

Wilson, A. G. and Pownall, C. M. (1976) 'A new representation of the urban system for modelling and for the study of micro-level interdependence', *Area*, 8, pp. 256–64.

Woldenburg, M. J. (1970) 'A structural taxonomy of spatial hierarchies', in J. Wood (2008) *How fiction works*, Jonathan Cape, London.

Zander, R. J. and Zander, B. (2000) *The art of possibility: transforming professional and personal life*, Harvard Business School Press, Boston.

Ziman, J. (1994) *Prometheus bound: science in a dynamic steady state*, Cambridge University Press, Cambridge.

Zohar, D. (1997) *Rewiring the corporate brain*, Berrett-Koehler, San Francisco.

Index